Stock Market Investing for Beginners

A Crash Course in Understanding the Basics of the Stock Market in Just 2 Hours

Heinrich Brevis

Table of Contents

Introduction 7

Chapter 1: What is the Stock Market? 10

    1.1 Understanding the Basics 13

    1.2 History of the Stock Market 15

    1.3 Why Invest in Stocks? 18

Chapter 2: How Does the Stock Market Work? 21

    2.1 Participants in the Stock Market 26

    2.2 Primary vs. Secondary Markets 29

    2.3 Order Types and Execution 32

Chapter 3: Getting Started with Stock Market Investing 36

    3.1 Setting Investment Goals 39

    3.2 Assessing Risk Tolerance 42

    3.3 Creating a Budget and Investment Plan 45

Chapter 4: Fundamental Analysis 50

    4.1 Understanding Financial Statements 53

    4.2 Evaluating Company Performance 56

    4.3 Key Financial Ratios 59

Chapter 5: Technical Analysis 63

    5.1 Introduction to Charts and Graphs 67

    5.2 Common Technical Indicators 71

    5.3 Trends and Patterns 73

Chapter 6: Types of Investments 78

    6.1 Stocks vs. Bonds vs. Mutual Funds 81

    6.2 ETFs and Index Funds 85

    6.3 Diversification Strategies 89

Chapter 7: Building Your Portfolio 93

    7.1 Choosing Stocks 96

    7.2 Portfolio Allocation Strategies 101

    7.3 Rebalancing and Monitoring 105

Chapter 8: Strategies for Success 109

    8.1 Long-Term vs. Short-Term Investing 112

8.2 Dollar-Cost Averaging 115

8.3 Managing Emotions and Risk.. 118

Chapter 9: Tools and Resources 122

9.1 Online Brokerages 125

9.2 Research Platforms.. 129

9.3 Investment Apps... 134

Chapter 10: Common Mistakes to Avoid... 139

10.1 Chasing Hot Stocks.. 141

10.2 Ignoring Fees and Taxes.. 144

10.3 Failing to Plan for the Long Term.. 148

Conclusion 152

Introduction

Welcome to "Stock Market Investing for Beginners: A Crash Course in Understanding the Basics of the Stock Market in Just 2 Hours." Whether you're looking to secure your financial future, grow your wealth, or simply gain a better understanding of the financial world, this book is your essential guide to navigating the complex yet rewarding world of stock market investing.

The stock market is often seen as a mysterious and intimidating realm, reserved for financial experts and Wall Street insiders. However, the truth is that anyone can learn to invest in stocks and potentially reap the benefits of long-term wealth accumulation. With the right knowledge and strategies, you can harness the power of the stock market to achieve your financial goals.

This book is specifically designed for beginners who are eager to dive into the world of stock market investing but may feel overwhelmed or unsure of where to start. In just two hours, you'll gain a solid foundation in the fundamental concepts, strategies, and tools necessary to begin your journey as a successful investor.

Throughout these pages, we'll cover everything you need to know to get started with confidence. From understanding what the stock market is and how it works to learn how to analyze stocks, build a diversified portfolio, and manage risk, each chapter is carefully crafted to provide clear, practical guidance.

Whether you're a recent college graduate, a working professional, or someone approaching retirement, the principles of stock market investing can be tailored to suit your unique financial circumstances and goals. By dedicating just a small fraction of your time to learning the basics, you'll be equipped with the knowledge and skills to make informed investment decisions for years to come.

So, are you ready to embark on this exciting journey? Let's dive in and unlock the world of opportunities that the stock market has to offer.

Happy investing!

Chapter 1: What is the Stock Market?

In the vast and intricate landscape of finance, few entities evoke as much fascination, curiosity, and sometimes fear, as the stock market. It's the beating heart of global capitalism, a place where fortunes are made and lost, where dreams soar and sometimes shatter. But what exactly is the stock market, and how does it function? Let's embark on a journey to demystify this enigmatic realm.

Origins and Evolution

The roots of the stock market trace back centuries, evolving from informal gatherings of traders to the sophisticated, electronically-driven exchanges of today. One of the earliest recorded instances of stock trading occurred in 17th-century Amsterdam, where merchants would gather to buy and sell shares of the Dutch East India Company. These gatherings laid the groundwork for what would eventually become the modern stock market.

Understanding Stocks

At its core, the stock market revolves around the buying and selling of stocks, also known as shares or equities. But what are stocks? Imagine you're a budding entrepreneur with a brilliant idea for a business, but you need capital to turn your vision into reality. Instead of borrowing money from a bank or seeking out investors individually, you decide to divide ownership of your company into shares, which you then sell to investors in exchange for funds. Each share represents a fractional ownership stake in the company, entitling its holder to a portion of its profits and assets.

Marketplaces and Exchanges

Stocks are traded on organized exchanges, which serve as platforms for buyers and sellers to come together and execute trades. Some of the most well-known exchanges include the New York Stock Exchange (NYSE) and the Nasdaq. These exchanges provide a centralized marketplace where stocks are listed, traded, and regulated. In addition to traditional exchanges, there are also electronic communication networks (ECNs) and over-the-counter (OTC) markets where stocks are traded outside of centralized exchanges.

Supply and Demand

At the heart of the stock market is the fundamental economic principle of supply and demand. The price of a stock is determined by the forces of supply and demand, with buyers and sellers constantly negotiating and adjusting their bids and offers. When there's high demand for a stock and limited supply, its price tends to rise. Conversely, when supply outweighs demand, prices fall. This delicate balance between supply and demand is what drives the fluctuations in stock prices.

Market Participants

The stock market is a dynamic ecosystem populated by a diverse array of participants, each with their own motivations and strategies. These participants include individual investors, institutional investors such as mutual funds and pension funds, hedge funds, investment banks, and market makers. Each group plays a unique role in shaping the dynamics of the market, from providing liquidity to influencing price movements.

Risks and Rewards

While the stock market offers the potential for substantial rewards, it also carries inherent risks. Prices can be volatile, subject to sudden swings driven by factors such as economic data releases, geopolitical events, and shifts in investor sentiment. Moreover, investing in individual stocks entails specific risks related to the performance of the underlying company, industry trends, and broader market conditions. However, for those willing to weather the ups and downs, the stock market can be a powerful wealth-building tool over the long term.

Regulation and Oversight

To ensure the integrity and stability of the stock market, regulatory bodies such as the Securities and Exchange Commission (SEC) in the United States play a crucial role in overseeing its operations. These regulators establish rules and regulations governing various aspects of the market, including disclosure requirements for publicly traded companies, insider trading restrictions, and measures to prevent market manipulation and fraud. By enforcing these regulations, regulators seek to maintain fair and orderly markets and protect investors' interests.

In summary, the stock market is a complex yet fascinating ecosystem that serves as the lifeblood of the global economy. It provides a mechanism for companies to raise capital, for investors to allocate their savings, and for economic activity to flourish. While the stock market may seem daunting at first glance, understanding its fundamentals can empower individuals to navigate its intricacies and participate in the wealth-building opportunities it offers. As we delve deeper into the world of finance, let us embrace the challenge of unraveling its mysteries and uncovering its hidden treasures.

1.1 Understanding the Basics

To embark on our journey into the realm of the stock market, it's essential to grasp the fundamental concepts that underpin its operations. In this section, we'll explore the basic building blocks of the stock market, laying the groundwork for a deeper understanding of its complexities.

What are Stocks?

At its core, the stock market revolves around the buying and selling of stocks, also known as shares or equities. But what exactly are stocks? Imagine you have a brilliant idea for a business but lack the funds to bring it to life. Instead of taking out loans or seeking individual investors, you decide to divide ownership of your company into shares, which you then sell to investors in exchange for capital. Each share represents a fractional ownership stake in the company, entitling its holder to a portion of its profits and assets.

Why Do Companies Issue Stocks?

Companies issue stocks for several reasons. Firstly, it's a way to raise capital to fund growth, expand operations, or invest in new projects. By selling shares to investors, companies can access a pool of capital without incurring debt. Secondly, issuing stocks allows companies to share ownership with a broader group of investors, spreading risk and aligning incentives. Additionally, publicly traded companies often use stocks as a form of currency for acquisitions or mergers, offering shares as consideration to the target company's shareholders.

How Do Stocks Trade?

Stocks are traded on organized exchanges, which serve as centralized marketplaces for buyers and sellers to come together and execute trades. Some of the most well-known exchanges include the New York Stock Exchange (NYSE) and the Nasdaq. These exchanges provide a platform for listing and trading stocks, as well as regulatory oversight to ensure fair and orderly markets. In addition to traditional exchanges, there are also electronic communication networks (ECNs) and over-the-counter (OTC) markets where stocks are traded outside of centralized exchanges.

What Determines Stock Prices?

The price of a stock is determined by the forces of supply and demand. When there's high demand for a stock and limited supply, its price tends to rise. Conversely, when supply outweighs demand, prices fall. Various factors influence supply and demand, including company performance, industry trends, economic conditions, investor sentiment, and geopolitical events. Additionally, market participants such as institutional investors, hedge funds, and individual traders contribute to price movements through their buying and selling activities.

In conclusion, understanding the basics of the stock market is essential for anyone looking to navigate its complexities and participate in its opportunities. Stocks represent ownership in companies, and their prices are driven by the forces of supply and demand. By grasping these fundamental concepts, investors can make informed decisions and navigate the dynamic landscape of the stock market with confidence. As we continue our exploration, let's delve deeper into the mechanisms that drive the world of finance and uncover the secrets to success in the stock market.

1.2 History of the Stock Market

To truly understand the stock market, it's vital to delve into its rich history, tracing its evolution from humble beginnings to the global powerhouse it is today. In this section, we'll embark on a journey through time, exploring the key milestones and events that have shaped the trajectory of the stock market.

Origins of Stock Trading

The origins of stock trading can be traced back to ancient civilizations, where informal markets and exchanges facilitated the trading of securities and commodities. However, it wasn't until the emergence of modern capitalism in the 17th century that the foundations of the stock market as we know it began to take shape.

Birth of Stock Exchanges

One of the earliest recorded instances of formal stock trading occurred in 17th-century Amsterdam, where merchants would gather at coffee houses to buy and sell shares of the Dutch East India Company and other ventures. These gatherings laid the groundwork for the establishment of the world's first official stock exchange, the Amsterdam Stock Exchange, which was founded in 1602.

Evolution of Stock Markets

Over the centuries, stock markets continued to evolve and expand, driven by advances in technology, changes in regulation, and shifts in global economic dynamics. The 18th and 19th centuries witnessed the rise of stock exchanges in major financial centers such as London, Paris, and New York, as well as the proliferation of joint-stock companies and the development of modern corporate finance.

Rise of Modern Exchanges

The 20th century brought further innovations to the stock market, including the advent of electronic trading, the rise of index funds and derivatives, and the globalization of financial markets. Major exchanges such as the New York Stock Exchange (NYSE) and the London Stock Exchange (LSE) emerged as leading hubs of financial activity, attracting investors from around the world.

Challenges and Transformations

The history of the stock market is also marked by periods of volatility, crisis, and transformation. From the Great Depression of the 1930s to the dot-com bubble of the late 1990s and the global financial crisis of 2008, the stock market has weathered its fair share of challenges. Each crisis has led to reforms, regulations, and innovations aimed at strengthening the resilience and integrity of the market.

In conclusion, the history of the stock market is a tale of innovation, resilience, and adaptation. From its humble origins in ancient marketplaces to its current status as a cornerstone of global finance, the stock market has undergone a remarkable journey of evolution and growth. By understanding its history, we gain valuable insights into the forces that have shaped the modern financial landscape and the challenges and opportunities that lie ahead. As we continue our exploration of the stock market, let us draw inspiration from its storied past and chart a course toward a prosperous future.

1.3 Why Invest in Stocks?

Investing in stocks has long been heralded as one of the most effective ways to build wealth and achieve financial security. In this section, we'll explore the compelling reasons why individuals and institutions choose to invest in stocks, highlighting the unique benefits and opportunities they offer.

Potential for Growth

One of the primary reasons investors are drawn to stocks is their potential for long-term growth. Historically, stocks have delivered higher returns compared to other asset classes such as bonds or cash equivalents. By investing in well-managed companies with strong growth prospects, investors can participate in the wealth creation that comes from business expansion, innovation, and market leadership.

Dividend Income

In addition to capital appreciation, stocks can also provide a source of regular income in the form of dividends. Many companies distribute a portion of their profits to shareholders in the form of dividends, providing a steady stream of income that can supplement other sources of revenue. Dividend-paying stocks are particularly attractive to income-oriented investors seeking to generate cash flow from their investments.

Diversification

Stocks offer investors the opportunity to diversify their portfolios and spread risk across different asset classes and industries. By investing in a broad range of stocks, investors can reduce their exposure to the risks associated with individual companies or sectors. Diversification is a key principle of risk management, helping investors mitigate the impact of market volatility and downturns.

Liquidity

Stocks are highly liquid assets, meaning they can be bought and sold easily on public exchanges. Unlike real estate or private equity investments, which may require time and effort to convert into cash, stocks can be traded quickly and efficiently. This liquidity provides investors with flexibility and the ability to adjust their portfolios in response to changing market conditions or investment objectives.

Ownership and Control

When you invest in stocks, you become a part-owner of the underlying companies, giving you a stake in their success and a voice in corporate governance matters. Shareholders have the right to vote on important company decisions, such as the election of board members, executive compensation, and major corporate initiatives. This ownership stake allows investors to exert influence and hold management accountable for their actions.

Stocks have historically served as a hedge against inflation, helping investors preserve the purchasing power of their wealth over time. Unlike fixed-income investments such as bonds, which may be eroded by inflation, stocks have the potential to generate returns that outpace rising prices. As companies increase their revenues and profits in response to inflationary pressures, stock prices may rise accordingly, providing investors with a natural inflation hedge.

In conclusion, investing in stocks offers a myriad of benefits that make them an attractive asset class for investors of all types. From the potential for long-term growth and dividend income to the benefits of diversification and liquidity, stocks provide investors with a powerful tool for building wealth and achieving their financial goals. By understanding the unique advantages of stocks and incorporating them into a well-balanced investment strategy, investors can unlock the full potential of the stock market and embark on a path towards financial prosperity.

Chapter 2: How Does the Stock Market Work?

In this chapter, we'll embark on a comprehensive exploration of the inner workings of the stock market. From the mechanics of buying and selling stocks to the factors that influence price movements, we'll unravel the complexities of this dynamic marketplace. By understanding how the stock market operates, investors can make informed decisions and navigate its intricacies with confidence.

Introduction to Market Mechanics

At its core, the stock market is a vast network of buyers and sellers who come together to trade stocks and other securities. The market operates through organized exchanges, electronic communication networks (ECNs), and over-the-counter (OTC) platforms, providing a platform for investors to buy and sell stocks.

Order Types

When investors wish to buy or sell stocks, they submit orders to the market specifying the price and quantity of shares they want to trade. There are several types of orders, including market orders, limit orders, and stop orders, each with its own characteristics and execution rules.

- **Market Orders**: Market orders are orders to buy or sell a stock at the best available price in the market. These orders are executed immediately at the prevailing market price, ensuring fast execution but potentially exposing investors to price fluctuations.

- **Limit Orders**: Limit orders allow investors to specify a maximum price to buy or a minimum price to sell a stock. These orders are only executed if the market price reaches the specified limit price, providing investors with control over the price at which their orders are executed.
- **Stop Orders**: Stop orders, also known as stop-loss orders, are orders to buy or sell a stock once it reaches a specified price, known as the stop price. These orders are typically used to limit losses or protect profits by triggering a trade when the stock price moves in a certain direction.

Market Participants

The stock market is populated by a diverse array of participants, each with their own motivations and strategies. These participants include individual investors, institutional investors such as mutual funds and pension funds, hedge funds, market makers, and high-frequency traders.

- **Individual Investors**: Individual investors, including retail traders and small-scale investors, buy and sell stocks for personal investment purposes, aiming to grow their wealth over time.
- **Institutional Investors**: Institutional investors are professional investors who manage large pools of capital on behalf of organizations such as mutual funds, pension funds, and insurance companies. These investors typically have access to extensive research and resources, allowing them to make informed investment decisions.

- **Market Makers**: Market makers are firms or individuals that facilitate trading in the stock market by providing liquidity and maintaining an orderly market. Market makers buy and sell stocks on their own behalf, profiting from the bid-ask spread—the difference between the buying and selling prices of a stock.

Price Discovery

One of the key functions of the stock market is price discovery, the process by which the market determines the fair value of stocks based on supply and demand. Prices are constantly changing as buyers and sellers negotiate and adjust their bids and offers, reflecting new information and market dynamics.

- **Bid and Ask Prices**: The bid price is the highest price at which buyers are willing to purchase a stock, while the ask price is the lowest price at which sellers are willing to sell. The difference between the bid and ask prices is known as the bid-ask spread, which represents the cost of executing a trade.
- **Market Depth**: Market depth refers to the level of liquidity in the market, or the number of buyers and sellers at various price levels. A deep market with high liquidity typically has tight bid-ask spreads and a greater number of shares available for trading.

Market Structure and Regulation

Exchanges and Trading Platforms

The stock market operates through a network of organized exchanges and electronic trading platforms, each with its own rules, regulations, and listing requirements. Some of the most well-known exchanges include the New York Stock Exchange (NYSE), the Nasdaq Stock Market, and the London Stock Exchange (LSE).

- **New York Stock Exchange (NYSE)**: The NYSE is the largest stock exchange in the world by market capitalization, with a long history dating back to 1792. It is known for its iconic trading floor and stringent listing requirements for companies.
- **Nasdaq Stock Market**: Nasdaq is a leading electronic exchange known for its technology-driven platform and focus on technology and growth-oriented companies. It is home to many of the world's largest technology firms, including Apple, Amazon, and Google.
- **Over-the-Counter (OTC) Markets**: In addition to organized exchanges, stocks can also be traded over-the-counter (OTC) through decentralized networks of broker-dealers. OTC markets provide a platform for trading stocks that are not listed on formal exchanges, including small-cap stocks and penny stocks.

Regulation and Oversight

The stock market is subject to extensive regulation and oversight by government agencies and regulatory bodies, aimed at ensuring fair and orderly markets and protecting investors' interests. In the United States, the Securities and Exchange Commission (SEC) is the primary regulatory agency responsible for overseeing the securities industry and enforcing federal securities laws.

- **Securities and Exchange Commission (SEC)**: The SEC regulates the securities industry, enforces securities laws, and oversees key market participants such as exchanges, broker-dealers, and investment advisers. It plays a crucial role in protecting investors and maintaining the integrity of the stock market.
- **Listing Requirements**: Exchanges impose listing requirements that companies must meet to have their stocks traded on their platforms. These requirements typically include minimum financial standards, corporate governance criteria, and disclosure obligations to ensure transparency and investor protection.

In conclusion, the stock market is a complex and dynamic marketplace where buyers and sellers come together to trade stocks and other securities. From the mechanics of order execution to the intricacies of price discovery, understanding how the stock market works is essential for investors looking to navigate its complexities and make informed investment decisions. By grasping the fundamental principles of market structure, regulation, and market dynamics, investors can unlock the full potential of the stock market and embark on a path toward financial success.

2.1 Participants in the Stock Market

In the intricate web of the stock market, various participants interact to create a dynamic marketplace. Understanding the roles and motivations of these participants is crucial for comprehending how the stock market operates. In this section, we'll delve into the diverse array of players who populate the stock market ecosystem.

Individual Investors

Individual investors, also known as retail investors, are everyday people who participate in the stock market with their personal funds. They buy and sell stocks through brokerage accounts, aiming to grow their wealth over time and achieve financial goals such as retirement savings, education funding, or wealth accumulation. Individual investors range from casual traders who dabble in the market occasionally to dedicated investors who actively manage their portfolios.

Institutional Investors

Institutional investors manage large pools of capital on behalf of organizations such as mutual funds, pension funds, insurance companies, and endowments. These sophisticated investors deploy substantial resources to conduct research, analyze markets, and make investment decisions. Institutional investors play a significant role in the stock market, accounting for a substantial portion of trading volume and influencing market trends through their buying and selling activities.

Mutual Funds

Mutual funds pool money from multiple investors to invest in a diversified portfolio of stocks, bonds, or other securities. Managed by professional fund managers, mutual funds offer investors a convenient way to access diversified investment strategies and achieve broad market exposure. Mutual funds come in various types, including equity funds that invest primarily in stocks, bond funds that invest in fixed-income securities, and balanced funds that maintain a mix of stocks and bonds.

Pension Funds

Pension funds manage retirement savings on behalf of employees, investing in a diversified portfolio of assets to generate returns and fund future pension obligations. These funds play a crucial role in providing financial security for retirees and are among the largest institutional investors in the stock market. Pension funds adopt long-term investment strategies aimed at achieving stable returns over time to meet their pension obligations.

Hedge Funds

Hedge funds are private investment vehicles that employ a wide range of strategies to generate returns for their investors. Unlike mutual funds, hedge funds are typically open only to accredited investors and have fewer regulatory constraints, allowing them to pursue more aggressive or complex investment strategies. Hedge funds often engage in active trading, employing techniques such as short selling, leverage, and derivatives to profit from market inefficiencies or mispricings.

Market Makers

Market makers are firms or individuals that facilitate trading in the stock market by providing liquidity and maintaining orderly markets. Acting as intermediaries between buyers and sellers, market makers continuously quote buy and sell prices for stocks, ensuring that there's always a counterparty available for trades. Market makers play a crucial role in enhancing market efficiency and reducing trading costs for investors by narrowing bid-ask spreads and absorbing excess supply or demand.

High-Frequency Traders (HFTs)

High-frequency traders are algorithmic trading firms that use sophisticated computer algorithms to execute trades at lightning-fast speeds. These traders leverage advanced technology and low-latency trading infrastructure to exploit short-term market inefficiencies and capitalize on price discrepancies. High-frequency trading accounts for a significant portion of trading volume in the stock market, with HFT firms engaging in rapid-fire trading across multiple exchanges and trading venues.

In conclusion, the stock market is a vibrant ecosystem populated by a diverse array of participants, each playing a unique role in shaping market dynamics and driving price movements. From individual investors seeking to grow their wealth to institutional investors managing large portfolios, and from market makers providing liquidity to high-frequency traders executing lightning-fast trades, the stock market thrives on the interactions and interplay of its participants. Understanding the motivations and strategies of these participants is essential for navigating the complexities of the stock market and making informed investment decisions. As we continue our exploration of the stock market, let's delve deeper into the roles and functions of these key players and uncover the secrets to success in this dynamic marketplace.

2.2 Primary vs. Secondary Markets

In the vast realm of the stock market, transactions take place in both primary and secondary markets, each serving distinct functions in the lifecycle of stocks and other securities. In this section, we'll explore the differences between these two markets and the roles they play in the process of buying and selling stocks.

Primary Market

The primary market is where newly issued securities are bought and sold for the first time, directly from the issuing company. In this market, companies raise capital by issuing new shares of stock through initial public offerings (IPOs) or additional offerings. The primary market enables companies to raise funds to finance business operations, expansion plans, or other strategic initiatives.

Initial Public Offerings (IPOs)

An initial public offering (IPO) is the process by which a company offers its shares to the public for the first time, transitioning from a privately-held entity to a publicly-traded company. During an IPO, the issuing company works with investment banks to underwrite and market the offering to investors. Once the shares are sold to investors, they begin trading on the secondary market exchanges.

Follow-On Offerings

In addition to IPOs, companies may issue additional shares of stock in follow-on offerings to raise additional capital. Follow-on offerings can take various forms, including secondary offerings, rights offerings, and private placements. These offerings provide existing shareholders with an opportunity to sell their shares or allow the company to raise capital for specific purposes, such as debt repayment or acquisition financing.

Secondary Market

The secondary market, also known as the aftermarket, is where existing securities are bought and sold among investors on organized exchanges or over-the-counter (OTC) platforms. Unlike the primary market, where securities are issued and sold directly by the issuing company, the secondary market involves trading among investors without the involvement of the issuing company.

Stock Exchanges

Stock exchanges such as the New York Stock Exchange (NYSE) and the Nasdaq serve as primary venues for trading stocks in the secondary market. These exchanges provide centralized platforms where buyers and sellers come together to execute trades, ensuring transparency, liquidity, and regulatory oversight. Stocks listed on exchanges are subject to listing requirements and regulatory scrutiny to maintain market integrity.

Over-the-Counter (OTC) Market

In addition to formal exchanges, stocks can also be traded over-the-counter (OTC) through decentralized networks of broker-dealers. OTC trading allows for more flexibility and accessibility, particularly for smaller companies that may not meet the listing requirements of formal exchanges. OTC markets provide a platform for trading stocks that are not listed on formal exchanges, including penny stocks and unlisted securities.

In conclusion, the primary and secondary markets play complementary roles in the process of buying and selling stocks. The primary market is where new securities are issued and sold by the issuing company, enabling companies to raise capital for growth and expansion. In contrast, the secondary market is where existing securities are traded among investors, providing liquidity and price discovery for investors seeking to buy or sell stocks. By understanding the functions and dynamics of both primary and secondary markets, investors can navigate the stock market with confidence and capitalize on investment opportunities across the lifecycle of stocks. As we continue our exploration of the stock market, let's delve deeper into the intricacies of primary and secondary market transactions and uncover the strategies for success in each.

2.3 Order Types and Execution

In the dynamic world of the stock market, investors have various order types at their disposal to execute trades effectively. Understanding these order types and their execution mechanisms is essential for navigating the complexities of the market and achieving desired outcomes. In this section, we'll explore the different types of orders investors can use and how they are executed in the stock market.

Market Orders

Market orders are among the simplest and most common types of orders used in the stock market. When investors place a market order, they are instructing their broker to buy or sell a security at the prevailing market price. Market orders are executed immediately, ensuring fast execution but providing no guarantee of price. As a result, market orders are particularly useful when investors prioritize speed of execution over price certainty.

Execution of Market Orders

When a market order is submitted, it is routed to the market where the security is traded, such as a stock exchange or an electronic trading platform. The order is then matched with existing orders in the market's order book, and the trade is executed at the best available price. Market orders are typically filled quickly, but the actual execution price may vary slightly from the quoted price due to market fluctuations and order size.

Limit Orders

Limit orders allow investors to specify a price at which they are willing to buy or sell a security. Unlike market orders, which prioritize speed of execution, limit orders provide price certainty but may not be executed immediately. If the market price reaches the specified limit price, the limit order is triggered, and the trade is executed at or better than the limit price.

Execution of Limit Orders

When a limit order is submitted, it remains on the order book until the market price reaches the specified limit price or better. Once the limit price is met, the order is activated, and the trade is executed at the limit price or a better price if available. If the limit order is not immediately executed, it may remain on the order book until it is filled or canceled by the investor.

Stop Orders

Stop orders, also known as stop-loss orders, are designed to protect investors from adverse price movements by triggering a trade when the market price reaches a specified level. If the market price reaches the stop price, the stop order is activated, and a market order is executed to buy or sell the security at the prevailing market price.

Execution of Stop Orders

When a stop order is submitted, it remains dormant until the market price reaches the specified stop price. Once the stop price is met, the stop order is triggered, and a market order is executed to buy or sell the security at the prevailing market price. Stop orders are commonly used by investors to limit losses or protect profits by automatically exiting a position when the market moves against them.

Market Depth and Order Execution

The execution of orders in the stock market is influenced by market depth or the level of liquidity available at various price levels. Orders with larger sizes may impact market depth and move prices, particularly in thinly traded securities or during periods of high volatility. Market makers play a crucial role in providing liquidity and maintaining orderly markets by quoting buy and sell prices for stocks and absorbing excess supply or demand.

In conclusion, order types and execution mechanisms are essential components of the stock market infrastructure, enabling investors to buy and sell securities efficiently. Market orders prioritize speed of execution but provide no guarantee of price, while limit orders offer price certainty but may not be executed immediately. Stop orders are used to protect investors from adverse price movements by triggering trades at specified price levels. By understanding the characteristics and execution mechanisms of different order types, investors can effectively navigate the stock market and achieve their investment objectives. As we continue our exploration of the stock market, let's delve deeper into the intricacies of order execution and uncover the strategies for success in executing trades.

Chapter 3: Getting Started with Stock Market Investing

In this chapter, we'll embark on a journey to demystify the process of getting started with stock market investing. Whether you're a novice investor or someone looking to enhance your investment knowledge, this chapter will provide you with the essential steps and strategies to begin your journey into the world of stock market investing.

Understanding Your Investment Goals

Before diving into the stock market, it's crucial to define your investment goals and objectives. Are you investing for retirement, wealth accumulation, education funding, or some other purpose? Understanding your investment goals will help you establish a clear roadmap and guide your investment decisions.

Educating Yourself

Investing in the stock market requires knowledge and understanding of fundamental concepts, investment strategies, and market dynamics. Take the time to educate yourself by reading books, articles, and online resources, attending seminars or workshops, and seeking guidance from experienced investors or financial advisors.

Assessing Your Risk Tolerance

Every investor has a unique risk tolerance, or willingness and ability to tolerate fluctuations in the value of their investments. Assessing your risk tolerance is essential for constructing a well-balanced investment portfolio that aligns with your comfort level and financial objectives. Consider factors such as your investment horizon, financial situation, and emotional temperament when evaluating your risk tolerance.

Building a Diversified Portfolio

Diversification is a key principle of successful investing, helping to spread risk across different asset classes, industries, and regions. Building a diversified portfolio can help mitigate the impact of market volatility and enhance long-term returns. Consider investing in a mix of stocks, bonds, mutual funds, exchange-traded funds (ETFs), and other asset classes to achieve diversification.

Choosing an Investment Strategy

There are various investment strategies to consider when investing in the stock market, ranging from passive index investing to active stock picking and everything in between. Evaluate different strategies based on your investment goals, risk tolerance, time horizon, and preferences. Whether you prefer a hands-on approach or a more passive strategy, choose an investment approach that aligns with your objectives and preferences.

Opening an Investment Account

Once you're ready to start investing, you'll need to open an investment account with a brokerage firm or investment platform. Choose a reputable brokerage that offers investment products, research tools, and customer support that meet your needs. Consider factors such as account fees, trading commissions, investment options, and account features when selecting a brokerage.

Conducting Research

Before making investment decisions, conduct thorough research on potential investment opportunities. Analyze the fundamentals of individual companies, including their financial performance, growth prospects, competitive positioning, and industry trends. Use research tools such as financial statements, analyst reports, company filings, and market data to inform your investment decisions.

Monitoring Your Investments

Investing in the stock market is an ongoing process that requires active monitoring and management of your investment portfolio. Stay informed about market developments, economic trends, and company news that may impact your investments. Regularly review your portfolio performance, assess your investment goals, and make adjustments as needed to stay on track towards achieving your objectives.

Seeking Professional Advice

If you're unsure about how to get started with stock market investing or if you need personalized guidance, consider seeking advice from a qualified financial advisor. A financial advisor can help you develop a tailored investment strategy, create a diversified portfolio, and navigate the complexities of the stock market. Look for a reputable advisor who has experience working with clients with similar financial goals and circumstances.

In conclusion, getting started with stock market investing requires careful planning, education, and diligence. By understanding your investment goals, assessing your risk tolerance, building a diversified portfolio, and choosing an investment strategy that aligns with your objectives, you can lay the foundation for a successful investment journey. Whether you're a novice investor or an experienced trader, the key is to stay informed, stay disciplined, and stay focused on your long-term goals. As you embark on your journey into the world of stock market investing, remember that patience, persistence, and prudent decision-making are essential ingredients for investment success.

3.1 Setting Investment Goals

Before venturing into the world of stock market investing, it's essential to define clear and achievable investment goals. Setting investment goals provides direction, focus, and a roadmap for your investment journey. In this section, we'll explore the importance of setting investment goals and provide guidance on how to establish goals that align with your financial aspirations.

Importance of Setting Investment Goals

Setting investment goals serves as the foundation of your investment strategy and provides clarity on what you aim to achieve through investing. Here are some key reasons why setting investment goals is crucial:

1. **Direction and Focus**: Investment goals help you define where you want to go and provide a clear direction for your investment journey. They help you stay focused on your objectives and avoid making impulsive investment decisions.
2. **Motivation and Discipline**: Having specific investment goals can motivate you to save and invest consistently over time. They provide a sense of purpose and discipline, encouraging you to stick to your investment plan even during market fluctuations or challenging times.
3. **Measure of Success**: Investment goals serve as benchmarks to evaluate your investment performance and measure your progress over time. By tracking your progress against your goals, you can determine whether your investment strategy is effective and make adjustments as needed.
4. **Tailored Approach**: Different investors have different financial aspirations, risk tolerances, and time horizons. Setting investment goals allows you to tailor your investment strategy to your unique circumstances and preferences, ensuring that your investments align with your needs and objectives.

How to Set Investment Goals

When setting investment goals, consider the following factors to ensure they are meaningful, realistic, and achievable:

1. **Define Your Objectives**: Start by clarifying what you want to achieve through investing. Are you investing for retirement, wealth accumulation, education funding, or another purpose? Be specific about your objectives and prioritize them based on their importance to you.

2. **Establish Timeframes**: Determine the timeframe for achieving each of your investment goals. Some goals, such as retirement savings, may have a long-term horizon, while others, such as saving for a down payment on a house, may have a shorter timeframe. Establishing timeframes will help you allocate resources and plan accordingly.

3. **Assess Risk Tolerance**: Understand your risk tolerance, or your willingness and ability to tolerate fluctuations in the value of your investments. Consider factors such as your financial situation, investment experience, and emotional temperament when assessing your risk tolerance. Align your investment goals with your risk tolerance to ensure a comfortable investing experience.

4. **Quantify Goals**: Quantify your investment goals by attaching specific numbers or targets to each objective. For example, if your goal is to accumulate a certain amount of wealth by retirement, specify the target amount you aim to achieve. Quantifying your goals makes them more tangible and actionable.

5. **Break Down Goals**: Break down larger goals into smaller, manageable milestones to make them less daunting and easier to track. For example, if your long-term goal is to retire comfortably,

break it down into smaller goals such as annual savings targets or net worth milestones to achieve along the way.

6. **Review and Adjust**: Regularly review your investment goals to ensure they remain relevant and aligned with your evolving financial circumstances and life priorities. As your situation changes or as you progress towards your goals, be prepared to adjust your goals accordingly to stay on track.

In conclusion, setting investment goals is a critical step in the investment planning process, providing direction, focus, and motivation for your investment journey. By defining clear and achievable goals, establishing realistic timeframes, assessing your risk tolerance, and quantifying your objectives, you can create a roadmap for success and make informed investment decisions that align with your financial aspirations. As you embark on your investment journey, remember to periodically review and adjust your goals to ensure they remain relevant and reflective of your evolving needs and priorities. With well-defined investment goals, you can navigate the complexities of the stock market with confidence and work towards achieving your long-term financial success.

3.2 Assessing Risk Tolerance

Assessing your risk tolerance is a crucial step in developing an investment strategy that aligns with your financial goals and preferences. Understanding how much risk you are willing and able to tolerate can help you construct a well-balanced investment portfolio that reflects your comfort level and objectives. In this section, we'll explore the importance of assessing risk tolerance and provide guidance on how to evaluate your risk tolerance effectively.

Importance of Assessing Risk Tolerance

Assessing risk tolerance is essential for several reasons:

1. **Aligning with Financial Goals**: Your risk tolerance should be in harmony with your investment objectives. By understanding your risk tolerance, you can ensure that your investment strategy is consistent with your financial goals and aspirations.
2. **Managing Emotions**: Investing involves uncertainty and volatility, which can evoke emotional responses such as fear, greed, and anxiety. Assessing your risk tolerance helps you understand how you might react to market fluctuations and make investment decisions based on logic rather than emotions.
3. **Balancing Risk and Return**: Risk and return are inherently linked in investing—higher potential returns typically come with higher levels of risk. Assessing your risk tolerance allows you to strike a balance between seeking returns and managing risk, ensuring that your investment portfolio reflects your risk-return preferences.
4. **Maintaining Long-Term Discipline**: Investing is a long-term endeavor, and staying invested through market ups and downs is crucial for achieving investment success. By assessing your risk tolerance, you can build a portfolio that you are comfortable holding through various market conditions, promoting long-term discipline and resilience.

How to Assess Risk Tolerance

Here are several approaches to assess your risk tolerance effectively:

1. **Risk Assessment Questionnaires**: Many financial institutions and online investment platforms offer risk assessment questionnaires that help investors gauge their risk tolerance. These questionnaires typically ask about factors such as investment experience, time horizon, financial goals, and willingness to accept fluctuations in portfolio value.

2. **Consider Investment Objectives**: Evaluate your investment objectives and time horizon to determine your risk tolerance. If you have long-term financial goals such as retirement savings and can withstand short-term market fluctuations, you may have a higher risk tolerance. Conversely, if you have short-term goals or a lower capacity to absorb losses, your risk tolerance may be lower.

3. **Evaluate Financial Situation**: Assess your financial situation, including income, expenses, savings, debts, and emergency funds, to understand your capacity to take on risk. Investors with stable incomes, ample savings, and manageable debt may have a higher risk tolerance compared to those with uncertain financial circumstances.

4. **Reflect on Emotional Response**: Consider how you might react to market volatility and fluctuations in the value of your investments. If the thought of losing money keeps you up at night or prompts you to make impulsive investment decisions, you may have a lower risk tolerance. Conversely, if you can remain calm and focused during market downturns, you may have a higher risk tolerance.

5. **Seek Professional Guidance**: If you're unsure about assessing your risk tolerance or need personalized advice, consider consulting a financial advisor. A qualified advisor can help you evaluate your risk tolerance, understand the implications of your investment strategy, and develop a portfolio that aligns with your goals and preferences.

In conclusion, assessing risk tolerance is a fundamental aspect of successful investing, helping investors understand their comfort level with uncertainty and volatility in the markets. By evaluating factors such as investment objectives, financial situation, emotional response to risk, and time horizon, investors can determine their risk tolerance and construct investment portfolios that reflect their unique preferences and objectives. As you assess your risk tolerance, remember that it's not just about avoiding losses—it's about finding the right balance between risk and return to achieve your financial goals while staying true to your comfort level. With a clear understanding of your risk tolerance, you can navigate the complexities of the stock market with confidence and build a resilient investment portfolio for the future.

3.3 Creating a Budget and Investment Plan

A budget and investment plan are essential tools for achieving your financial goals and building wealth over time. By creating a budget, you can manage your expenses, save money, and allocate funds for investing. An investment plan helps you outline your investment objectives, strategies, and asset allocation to make informed decisions about where to invest your money. In this section, we'll explore the importance of creating a budget and investment plan and provide guidance on how to develop them effectively.

Importance of Creating a Budget

A budget serves as the foundation of your financial plan and provides a roadmap for managing your money effectively. Here's why creating a budget is essential:

1. **Expense Management**: A budget helps you track your income and expenses, allowing you to identify areas where you can cut costs, eliminate unnecessary spending, and save more money for investing.
2. **Savings Allocation**: By allocating a portion of your income to savings and investments, you can build an emergency fund, achieve short-term financial goals, and accumulate wealth over time through the power of compounding.
3. **Debt Management**: A budget enables you to prioritize debt repayment by allocating funds towards paying off high-interest debt such as credit cards or loans. By reducing debt, you can free up more money for saving and investing in the future.
4. **Goal Setting**: A budget helps you set specific financial goals, such as saving for a down payment on a house, funding a child's education, or preparing for retirement. By breaking down larger goals into smaller, manageable targets, you can stay focused and motivated to achieve them.

How to Create a Budget

Follow these steps to create a budget that aligns with your financial goals and priorities:

1. **Calculate Your Income**: Start by calculating your total monthly income, including salaries, wages, bonuses, and any other sources of income.
2. **Track Your Expenses**: Track your monthly expenses by categorizing them into essential expenses (e.g., housing, groceries, utilities) and discretionary expenses (e.g., dining out,

entertainment, travel). Use tools such as budgeting apps or spreadsheets to track your expenses accurately.

3. **Set Spending Targets**: Determine how much you want to allocate towards each expense category based on your financial priorities and goals. Aim to prioritize essential expenses while minimizing discretionary spending to free up more money for saving and investing.

4. **Establish Savings Goals**: Set specific savings goals, such as building an emergency fund, saving for a major purchase, or investing for retirement. Allocate a portion of your income towards savings each month to work towards achieving these goals.

5. **Review and Adjust**: Regularly review your budget to track your progress, identify areas for improvement, and make adjustments as needed. Be flexible and adaptable, especially during times of change or unexpected expenses.

Importance of Creating an Investment Plan

An investment plan outlines your investment objectives, strategies, and asset allocation to guide your investment decisions. Here's why creating an investment plan is crucial:

1. **Goal Alignment**: An investment plan ensures that your investment strategy aligns with your financial goals, risk tolerance, and time horizon. It provides a framework for making informed decisions about where to invest your money to achieve your objectives.

2. **Diversification**: By diversifying your investment portfolio across different asset classes, sectors, and geographic regions, an investment plan helps reduce risk and volatility while potentially enhancing returns over the long term.

3. **Risk Management**: An investment plan includes strategies for managing investment risk, such as asset allocation, diversification, and periodic rebalancing. It helps you stay disciplined and avoid emotional decision-making during market fluctuations.
4. **Monitoring and Evaluation**: An investment plan establishes criteria for monitoring the performance of your investments and evaluating their effectiveness in achieving your goals. It allows you to make adjustments to your portfolio as needed and stay on track toward financial success.

How to Create an Investment Plan

Follow these steps to create an investment plan that suits your financial objectives and risk tolerance:

1. **Define Your Investment Objectives**: Clarify your investment goals, such as retirement savings, wealth accumulation, or funding a major purchase. Determine your investment time horizon and risk tolerance to guide your investment strategy.
2. **Determine Asset Allocation**: Decide how to allocate your investment portfolio across different asset classes, such as stocks, bonds, cash, and alternative investments. Consider your risk tolerance, investment goals, and market conditions when determining asset allocation.
3. **Select Investment Vehicles**: Choose specific investment vehicles, such as individual stocks, mutual funds, exchange-traded funds (ETFs), or real estate, to implement your investment strategy. Evaluate factors such as fees, performance, and risk characteristics when selecting investments.

4. **Implement Risk Management Strategies**: Incorporate risk management strategies into your investment plan, such as diversification, asset allocation, and periodic rebalancing. Adjust your portfolio as needed to maintain alignment with your risk tolerance and investment objectives.
5. **Monitor and Reevaluate**: Regularly monitor the performance of your investments and evaluate their alignment with your investment plan. Make adjustments to your portfolio as needed based on changes in market conditions, financial goals, or personal circumstances.

In conclusion, creating a budget and investment plan are essential steps in achieving your financial goals and building wealth over time. A budget helps you manage your expenses, save money, and allocate funds for investing, while an investment plan guides your investment decisions and helps you achieve your long-term objectives. By establishing clear financial goals, tracking your income and expenses, and developing a well-defined investment strategy, you can take control of your finances and work towards achieving financial success. As you embark on your journey toward financial independence, remember that discipline, patience, and consistency are key to long-term investment success.

Chapter 4: Fundamental Analysis

In the dynamic world of finance and investment, understanding fundamental analysis is akin to having a compass in a dense forest – it guides you through the intricacies of the market, helping you navigate through the noise and make informed decisions. In this chapter, we delve deep into the essence of fundamental analysis, its principles, methods, and how it can empower investors to unearth valuable opportunities.

The Essence of Fundamental Analysis

At its core, fundamental analysis is a method used by investors to evaluate the intrinsic value of a security by examining related economic, financial, and qualitative factors. Unlike technical analysis, which focuses on historical price movements and patterns, fundamental analysis delves into the underlying factors that drive the value of an asset.

Principles of Fundamental Analysis

1. Understanding the Business

Fundamental analysis begins with a thorough understanding of the business behind the stock. This involves studying the company's business model, revenue streams, products or services, competitive advantages, and market positioning. By gaining insights into the fundamentals of the business, investors can assess its growth potential and future prospects.

2. Financial Statements Analysis

A critical aspect of fundamental analysis is the examination of a company's financial statements – including the balance sheet, income statement, and cash flow statement. These documents provide valuable information about the company's financial health, profitability, liquidity, and solvency. By analyzing key financial ratios and metrics, investors can gauge the company's performance and stability.

3. Economic and Industry Analysis

In addition to analyzing individual companies, fundamental analysts also assess broader economic and industry trends. Factors such as GDP growth, inflation rates, interest rates, and industry dynamics can significantly impact the performance of businesses. By staying abreast of macroeconomic indicators and industry developments, investors can better anticipate market trends and adjust their investment strategies accordingly.

4. Qualitative Factors Evaluation

Beyond numbers and financial metrics, fundamental analysis encompasses qualitative factors such as management quality, corporate governance, brand reputation, and competitive advantages. These intangible aspects can play a crucial role in shaping a company's long-term success and market valuation. By conducting qualitative analysis, investors can gain deeper insights into the intrinsic value of a stock.

Methods of Fundamental Analysis

1. Value Investing

Popularized by legendary investors like Benjamin Graham and Warren Buffett, value investing is a fundamental analysis strategy that involves identifying undervalued stocks trading below their intrinsic value. Value investors seek companies with strong fundamentals, sound business models, and attractive growth prospects, but whose stock prices do not fully reflect their true worth. By buying these undervalued stocks and holding them for the long term, investors aim to generate substantial returns as the market eventually recognizes their true value.

2. Growth Investing

In contrast to value investing, growth investing focuses on identifying companies with high growth potential and investing in them early in their growth trajectory. Growth investors look for companies with strong earnings growth, innovative products or services, expanding market share, and competitive advantages. By investing in these growth-oriented companies, investors aim to capitalize on their potential for above-average returns over time.

3. Dividend Investing

Dividend investing revolves around selecting stocks that offer attractive dividend yields and a track record of consistent dividend payments.

Dividend-paying companies are often mature, stable businesses with strong cash flows and a commitment to returning capital to shareholders. Dividend investors seek to build a portfolio of income-generating stocks that provide regular dividend income and the potential for capital appreciation over the long term.

Fundamental analysis is a cornerstone of intelligent investing, providing investors with a systematic framework for evaluating securities and making informed decisions. By understanding the principles and methods of fundamental analysis, investors can uncover valuable investment opportunities, mitigate risks, and achieve their financial goals. Whether you're a novice investor or a seasoned professional, mastering the art of fundamental analysis is essential for success in the dynamic world of finance and investment.

4.1 Understanding Financial Statements

Financial statements are the bedrock of fundamental analysis, offering a snapshot of a company's financial health and performance. In this section, we'll break down the components of financial statements and explore how investors can interpret them to gain insights into a company's operations and prospects.

Components of Financial Statements

1. Balance Sheet

The balance sheet provides a snapshot of a company's financial position at a specific point in time. It consists of three main sections:

- **Assets**: These are resources owned by the company, such as cash, inventory, property, and equipment.
- **Liabilities**: These are obligations owed by the company, including loans, accounts payable, and accrued expenses.
- **Shareholders' Equity**: This represents the residual value of assets after deducting liabilities. It includes common stock, retained earnings, and additional paid-in capital.

2. Income Statement

The income statement, also known as the profit and loss statement, summarizes a company's revenues, expenses, and net income over a specific period. Key components include:

- **Revenue**: The total amount of money earned from selling goods or services.
- **Expenses**: The costs incurred in generating revenue, such as cost of goods sold, operating expenses, and taxes.
- **Net Income**: The difference between revenue and expenses, indicating the company's profitability.

3. Cash Flow Statement

The cash flow statement tracks the inflows and outflows of cash during a given period, categorizing them into three main sections:

- **Operating Activities**: Cash flows from day-to-day business operations, such as sales, purchases, and operating expenses.
- **Investing Activities**: Cash flows from buying or selling assets, such as property, equipment, or investments.
- **Financing Activities**: Cash flows from borrowing or repaying debt, issuing or repurchasing stock, and paying dividends.

Interpreting Financial Statements

1. Liquidity

Liquidity refers to a company's ability to meet its short-term obligations with available cash and assets that can be quickly converted into cash. Investors assess liquidity by examining metrics such as the current ratio (current assets divided by current liabilities) and the quick ratio (liquid assets divided by current liabilities).

2. Solvency

Solvency measures a company's ability to meet its long-term financial obligations. Investors evaluate solvency by analyzing metrics such as the debt-to-equity ratio (total debt divided by shareholders' equity) and the interest coverage ratio (earnings before interest and taxes divided by interest expense).

3. Profitability

Profitability measures a company's ability to generate earnings relative to its expenses and investments. Investors evaluate profitability using metrics such as gross profit margin (gross profit divided by revenue), operating profit margin (operating income divided by revenue), and return on equity (net income divided by shareholders' equity).

Understanding financial statements is essential for investors seeking to make informed decisions in the stock market. By analyzing the balance sheet, income statement, and cash flow statement, investors can gain valuable insights into a company's financial health, performance, and prospects. Whether you're a novice investor or a seasoned professional, mastering the art of interpreting financial statements is key to successful fundamental analysis and investment decision-making.

4.2 Evaluating Company Performance

Assessing a company's performance is a critical aspect of fundamental analysis, allowing investors to gauge its financial health, profitability, and growth prospects. In this section, we'll discuss key metrics and methods for evaluating company performance.

Key Performance Metrics

1. Revenue Growth

Revenue growth reflects the increase in a company's sales over a specific period. A consistently growing top line indicates strong demand for the company's products or services and is often a sign of a healthy business.

2. Profitability Ratios

Profitability ratios measure a company's ability to generate earnings relative to its expenses and investments. Key profitability metrics include:

- **Gross Profit Margin**: The percentage of revenue that exceeds the cost of goods sold, indicating the efficiency of production or service delivery.
- **Net Profit Margin**: The percentage of revenue that remains as net income after deducting all expenses, taxes, and interest payments.

3. Return on Investment (ROI)

ROI measures the efficiency of an investment relative to its cost. It is calculated by dividing the net profit or benefit from the investment by the initial cost or investment amount, expressed as a percentage. A higher ROI indicates better investment efficiency.

4. Earnings Per Share (EPS)

EPS measures the portion of a company's profit allocated to each outstanding share of common stock. It is calculated by dividing the company's net income by the total number of outstanding shares. EPS growth is often a key indicator of a company's profitability and shareholder value.

Fundamental Analysis Methods

1. Comparative Analysis

Comparative analysis involves benchmarking a company's performance against its peers or industry averages. By comparing key financial metrics such as revenue growth, profitability ratios, and market share, investors can assess how well a company is performing relative to its competitors.

2. Trend Analysis

Trend analysis involves analyzing a company's performance over multiple periods to identify patterns and trends. By examining historical financial data and performance metrics, investors can discern whether a company's performance is improving, deteriorating, or remaining stable over time.

3. Ratio Analysis

Ratio analysis involves calculating and interpreting various financial ratios to assess different aspects of a company's performance. Common ratios used in fundamental analysis include:

- **Liquidity Ratios**: Measure a company's ability to meet its short-term obligations.
- **Solvency Ratios**: Measure a company's ability to meet its long-term financial obligations.
- **Efficiency Ratios**: Measure a company's ability to manage its assets, liabilities, and working capital effectively.

Evaluating company performance is essential for investors seeking to make informed investment decisions. By analyzing key performance metrics and employing fundamental analysis methods such as comparative analysis, trend analysis, and ratio analysis, investors can gain valuable insights into a company's financial health, profitability, and growth potential. Whether you're a beginner or seasoned investor, mastering the art of evaluating company performance is crucial for successful investing in the stock market.

4.3 Key Financial Ratios

Financial ratios are powerful tools that enable investors to assess a company's financial health, performance, and valuation. In this section, we'll explore some of the key financial ratios commonly used in fundamental analysis.

1. Liquidity Ratios

a. Current Ratio

The current ratio measures a company's ability to meet its short-term obligations with its short-term assets. It is calculated by dividing current assets by current liabilities. A ratio above 1 indicates that the company has more current assets than current liabilities, suggesting good liquidity.

b. Quick Ratio (Acid-Test Ratio)

The quick ratio, also known as the acid-test ratio, is a more stringent measure of liquidity that excludes inventory from current assets. It is calculated by dividing quick assets (current assets minus inventory) by current liabilities. A higher quick ratio indicates greater liquidity and a lower reliance on inventory to meet short-term obligations.

2. Solvency Ratios

a. Debt-to-Equity Ratio

The debt-to-equity ratio measures the proportion of a company's financing that comes from debt compared to equity. It is calculated by dividing total debt by shareholders' equity. A high debt-to-equity ratio may indicate that a company is heavily leveraged and could be at risk of financial distress.

b. Interest Coverage Ratio

The interest coverage ratio measures a company's ability to meet its interest obligations with its earnings before interest and taxes (EBIT). It is calculated by dividing EBIT by interest expense. A higher interest coverage ratio indicates that a company has sufficient earnings to cover its interest payments comfortably.

3. Profitability Ratios

a. Gross Profit Margin

The gross profit margin measures the percentage of revenue that exceeds the cost of goods sold (COGS). It is calculated by dividing gross profit by revenue. A higher gross profit margin indicates that a company is effectively managing its production costs.

b. Net Profit Margin

The net profit margin measures the percentage of revenue that remains as net income after deducting all expenses, taxes, and interest payments. It is calculated by dividing net income by revenue. A higher net profit margin indicates greater profitability and efficiency in managing expenses.

4. Efficiency Ratios

a. Inventory Turnover Ratio

The inventory turnover ratio measures how many times a company's inventory is sold and replaced over a specific period. It is calculated by dividing the cost of goods sold by average inventory. A higher inventory turnover ratio suggests that a company is efficiently managing its inventory and generating sales.

b. Accounts Receivable Turnover Ratio

The accounts receivable turnover ratio measures how efficiently a company is collecting payments from its customers. It is calculated by dividing credit sales by average accounts receivable. A higher accounts receivable turnover ratio indicates that a company is effectively managing its accounts receivable and converting sales into cash quickly.

Key financial ratios provide valuable insights into a company's financial health, performance, and efficiency. By analyzing liquidity ratios, solvency ratios, profitability ratios, and efficiency ratios, investors can assess various aspects of a company's operations and make informed investment decisions. Whether you're a novice investor or seasoned professional, mastering the interpretation of key financial ratios is essential for successful fundamental analysis and investment success in the stock market.

Chapter 5: Technical Analysis

In the realm of financial markets, technical analysis stands as a beacon, guiding investors through the labyrinth of price movements and market trends. This chapter delves deep into the world of technical analysis, unraveling its principles, methods, and tools that empower traders to decipher the language of the market.

The Essence of Technical Analysis

Technical analysis is a method of evaluating securities by analyzing statistical trends gathered from trading activity, such as price movement and volume. Unlike fundamental analysis, which focuses on examining the intrinsic value of assets, technical analysis revolves around the belief that historical price data can forecast future price movements. At its core, technical analysis is grounded in the principle that market trends tend to repeat themselves due to human behavior, allowing traders to identify patterns and make informed trading decisions.

Principles of Technical Analysis

1. Price Discounts Everything

One of the fundamental principles of technical analysis is that all relevant information regarding security, including its fundamentals, market sentiment, and external factors, is already reflected in its price. Therefore, rather than analyzing external factors individually, technical analysts focus solely on price action and its patterns to predict future movements.

2. Price Moves in Trends

Another key principle of technical analysis is that price movements tend to follow trends, whether upward, downward, or sideways. By identifying and analyzing these trends, traders can capitalize on the momentum and direction of the market to enter and exit positions profitably.

3. History Tends to Repeat Itself

Technical analysts believe that historical price data often repeats itself due to the collective behavior of market participants. As a result, patterns that have proven to be reliable indicators in the past are likely to recur in the future. By recognizing these patterns, traders can anticipate potential price movements and adjust their trading strategies accordingly.

Methods of Technical Analysis

1. Chart Patterns

Chart patterns are graphical representations of price movements that occur repeatedly in the market. Some of the most common chart patterns include:

- **Trendlines**: Lines drawn along the highs and lows of price movements to identify the direction of the trend.
- **Support and Resistance Levels**: Price levels where buying or selling pressure is concentrated, creating barriers that prices tend to bounce off or reverse from.
- **Reversal Patterns**: Patterns that signal a potential reversal in the prevailing trend, such as head and shoulders, double tops, and double bottoms.
- **Continuation Patterns**: Patterns that suggest a continuation of the prevailing trend, such as flags, pennants, and triangles.

2. Technical Indicators

Technical indicators are mathematical calculations based on price and volume data that help traders analyze market trends and momentum. Some popular technical indicators include:

- **Moving Averages**: Averages of past price data that smooth out fluctuations and help identify the direction of the trend.
- **Relative Strength Index (RSI)**: A momentum oscillator that measures the speed and change of price movements to determine overbought or oversold conditions.
- **Moving Average Convergence Divergence (MACD)**: A trend-following momentum indicator that shows the relationship between two moving averages of a security's price.
- **Bollinger Bands**: Bands plotted above and below a simple moving average to indicate volatility and potential price reversals.

3. Volume Analysis

Volume analysis examines the trading volume accompanying price movements to gauge the strength and validity of trends. High volume often confirms the significance of price movements, indicating strong market participation and conviction.

Practical Applications of Technical Analysis

1. Trend Following

One of the most common strategies employed by technical traders is trend following, where traders seek to profit from the continuation of established trends. By identifying and riding trends using trendlines, moving averages, and other technical indicators, traders aim to capitalize on momentum and maximize profits.

2. Counter-Trend Trading

Contrary to trend following, counter-trend trading involves identifying potential reversals in the market and trading against the prevailing trend. This strategy often relies on recognizing overbought or oversold conditions using indicators like RSI and divergence patterns to anticipate trend reversals and profit from short-term corrections.

3. Breakout Trading

Breakout trading involves entering positions when the price breaks through key support or resistance levels, signaling the potential for a significant price movement. Traders use chart patterns like triangles and rectangles, coupled with volume analysis, to identify breakout opportunities and capitalize on explosive price moves.

Technical analysis is a powerful tool that empowers traders to navigate the complexities of financial markets and make informed trading decisions. By analyzing price action, chart patterns, technical indicators, and volume data, traders can gain valuable insights into market trends, momentum, and potential price movements. Whether you're a novice trader or a seasoned professional, mastering the art of technical analysis is essential for success in the dynamic world of trading and investing.

5.1 Introduction to Charts and Graphs

In the world of technical analysis, charts and graphs serve as the canvas upon which traders paint their understanding of market dynamics and price movements. In this section, we embark on a journey into the realm of charts and graphs, exploring their significance, types, and practical applications in analyzing financial markets.

The Significance of Charts and Graphs

Charts and graphs are indispensable tools for visualizing and interpreting market data. They provide a graphical representation of price movements, trends, and patterns over time, allowing traders to identify opportunities and make informed decisions. By condensing complex numerical data into visual formats, charts, and graphs facilitates quick analysis and enhance comprehension of market dynamics.

Types of Charts and Graphs

1. Line Charts

Line charts are perhaps the simplest and most commonly used type of chart in technical analysis. They plot the closing prices of a security over a specific period, connecting each data point with a line. Line charts provide a clear visualization of price trends and are ideal for identifying long-term patterns and trends.

2. Bar Charts

Bar charts display price movements using vertical bars, with each bar representing a specific time period (e.g., day, week, month). The height of the bar indicates the price range between the high and low prices during that period, while horizontal lines on the left and right sides represent the opening and closing prices, respectively. Bar charts provide more detailed information than line charts and are useful for analyzing price volatility and trading activity.

3. Candlestick Charts

Candlestick charts originated in Japan and have become a popular tool in technical analysis due to their ability to convey a wealth of information in a single visual. Each candlestick represents the price movement of a security over a specific period, typically a day. The body of the candlestick illustrates the price range between the opening and closing prices, while the wicks (or shadows) above and below the body indicate the high and low prices, respectively. Candlestick patterns provide insights into market sentiment and are widely used for identifying trend reversals and price patterns.

4. Point and Figure Charts

Point and figure charts are unique in that they focus solely on price movements, disregarding time intervals. Instead of using bars or candlesticks, point and figure charts use Xs and Os to represent price changes. Xs denote rising prices, while Os represent falling prices. Point and figure charts filter out minor price fluctuations and focus on significant price movements, making them particularly useful for identifying support and resistance levels and trend reversals.

Practical Applications of Charts and Graphs

1. Trend Identification

Charts and graphs play a crucial role in identifying trends in the market. Whether using line charts, bar charts, or candlestick charts, traders analyze price movements over time to identify the direction of the trend – whether it's upward, downward, or sideways. Trend identification is essential for making informed trading decisions and capitalizing on momentum.

2. Pattern Recognition

Patterns are recurring formations in price movements that often precede significant market moves. Charts and graphs enable traders to recognize and interpret these patterns, such as head and shoulders, double tops, triangles, and flags. By identifying these patterns, traders can anticipate potential price movements and adjust their trading strategies accordingly.

3. Support and Resistance Levels

Support and resistance levels are key price levels where buying or selling pressure is concentrated, creating barriers that prices tend to bounce off or reverse from. Charts and graphs help traders identify these levels visually and anticipate potential price reactions. Support and resistance levels provide valuable reference points for setting entry and exit points, as well as stop-loss orders.

Charts and graphs are indispensable tools for traders seeking to navigate the complexities of financial markets. Whether using line charts, bar charts, candlestick charts, or point and figure charts, traders leverage visual representations of price movements to identify trends, patterns, and key support and resistance levels. By mastering the art of chart analysis, traders can enhance their decision-making process and gain a competitive edge in the dynamic world of trading and investing.

5.2 Common Technical Indicators

Technical indicators are invaluable tools for traders, providing insights into market trends, momentum, and potential price movements. In this section, we explore some of the most widely used technical indicators in the realm of technical analysis.

1. Moving Averages

Moving averages are among the most fundamental and versatile technical indicators used by traders. They smooth out price data to create a single flowing line, representing the average price over a specified period. The two most common types of moving averages are:

- **Simple Moving Average (SMA)**: Calculates the average price over a specific number of periods equally.
- **Exponential Moving Average (EMA)**: Gives more weight to recent prices, making it more responsive to recent price changes.

Moving averages help traders identify trends, support and resistance levels, and potential trend reversals. Crossovers between different moving averages, such as the golden cross (short-term moving average crossing above a long-term moving average) and death cross (short-term moving average crossing below a long-term moving average), are often used as trading signals.

2. Relative Strength Index (RSI)

The Relative Strength Index (RSI) is a momentum oscillator that measures the speed and change of price movements. It oscillates between 0 and 100 and is typically plotted below the price chart. RSI values above 70 indicate overbought conditions, suggesting that the asset may be due for a correction, while RSI values below 30 indicate oversold conditions, signaling a potential buying opportunity. Traders use RSI to identify divergences between price and momentum, as well as overbought or oversold conditions.

3. Moving Average Convergence Divergence (MACD)

The Moving Average Convergence Divergence (MACD) is a trend-following momentum indicator that consists of two lines: the MACD line and the signal line. The MACD line is calculated by subtracting the 26-period exponential moving average from the 12-period exponential moving average, while the signal line is a 9-period exponential moving average of the MACD line. Traders look for crossovers between the MACD line and the signal line as potential buy or sell signals. Additionally, the MACD histogram, which represents the difference between the MACD line and the signal line, helps traders visualize the strength of the trend.

4. Bollinger Bands

Bollinger Bands are volatility indicators that consist of a simple moving average (usually 20 periods) and two standard deviation bands plotted above and below the moving average. The width of the bands expands and contracts based on market volatility. Traders use Bollinger Bands to identify overbought and oversold conditions when prices touch or exceed the bands, as well as to gauge the potential for price reversals when the bands contract after a period of volatility.

5. Stochastic Oscillator

The Stochastic Oscillator is another momentum oscillator that measures the location of a security's closing price relative to its price range over a specific period. It oscillates between 0 and 100 and consists of two lines: the %K line and the %D line. Traders look for crossovers and divergences between the %K and %D lines to identify potential buy or sell signals. Additionally, overbought and oversold conditions are indicated by extreme readings above 80 and below 20, respectively.

Technical indicators are essential tools for traders seeking to analyze market trends, momentum, and potential price movements. Whether using moving averages, oscillators, or volatility indicators, traders leverage these tools to make informed trading decisions and identify profitable opportunities in the dynamic world of financial markets. By mastering the application of common technical indicators, traders can enhance their trading strategies and gain a competitive edge in the pursuit of trading success.

5.3 Trends and Patterns

Understanding trends and patterns is crucial for traders seeking to navigate the complex landscape of financial markets. In this section, we explore the concepts of trends and patterns, how they manifest in price movements, and their significance in technical analysis.

Trends

Trends are the directional movements of prices over time, reflecting the general sentiment of market participants. There are three primary types of trends:

1. Uptrend

An uptrend is characterized by a series of higher highs and higher lows, indicating a bullish bias in the market. In an uptrend, buyers outnumber sellers, leading to sustained upward price movements. Traders and investors seek to capitalize on uptrends by buying assets with the expectation of continued price appreciation.

2. Downtrend

A downtrend is marked by a sequence of lower highs and lower lows, signaling a bearish sentiment in the market. In a downtrend, sellers dominate the market, driving prices lower over time. Traders and investors may short-sell assets or adopt defensive strategies to mitigate losses during downtrends.

3. Sideways (or Range-bound) Trend

A sideways trend, also known as a range-bound market, occurs when prices fluctuate within a relatively narrow price range, without establishing a clear directional bias. In a sideways trend, buying and selling pressure is roughly balanced, resulting in horizontal price movements. Traders may employ range-bound trading strategies, buying at support levels and selling at resistance levels, until a breakout or breakdown occurs.

Patterns

Patterns are recurring formations in price movements that provide insights into market sentiment and potential future price movements. Some common patterns observed in technical analysis include:

1. Head and Shoulders

The head and shoulders pattern is a reversal pattern that consists of three peaks – a higher peak (head) flanked by two lower peaks (shoulders) – with a neckline connecting the lows of the two troughs. A head and shoulders pattern signals a potential trend reversal from bullish to bearish, with the neckline serving as a key level of support-turned-resistance.

2. Double Top and Double Bottom

The double-top pattern occurs when prices form two consecutive peaks at approximately the same level, separated by a trough. Conversely, the double bottom pattern occurs when prices form two consecutive troughs at approximately the same level, separated by a peak. Double-top patterns indicate a potential trend reversal from bullish to bearish, while double-bottom patterns suggest a reversal from bearish to bullish.

3. Flags and Pennants

Flags and pennants are continuation patterns that occur after a strong price movement, representing brief pauses or consolidation periods before the trend resumes. Flags are characterized by parallel trendlines sloping against the prevailing trend, while pennants are marked by converging trendlines. Both patterns signal a temporary pause in the trend, followed by a continuation in the same direction.

4. Triangles

Triangles are consolidation patterns characterized by converging trendlines, indicating a period of indecision in the market. There are three main types of triangles:

- **Symmetrical Triangle**: Both trendlines converge at a similar angle, with no clear bias in price direction.

- **Ascending Triangle**: The upper trendline is horizontal, while the lower trendline slopes upwards, and indicating potential bullish continuation.
- **Descending Triangle**: The lower trendline is horizontal, while the upper trendline slopes downwards, and suggesting a potential bearish continuation.

Trends and patterns are integral components of technical analysis, providing valuable insights into market dynamics and potential price movements. By understanding and identifying trends, traders can capitalize on directional price movements, while recognizing and interpreting patterns enables traders to anticipate trend reversals and continuation. Mastery of trends and patterns empowers traders to make informed decisions and navigate the ever-changing landscape of financial markets with confidence.

Chapter 6: Types of Investments

Investing is the art of allocating resources with the expectation of generating future returns. In this chapter, we explore various types of investments, ranging from traditional assets to alternative investments, each offering unique characteristics and potential opportunities for investors.

1. Stocks

Stocks, also known as equities, represent ownership stakes in publicly traded companies. When investors buy stocks, they acquire shares of ownership in the company and become entitled to a portion of its profits through dividends (if paid) and potential capital appreciation. Stocks are considered one of the primary vehicles for long-term wealth accumulation, offering the potential for significant returns but also carrying inherent risks due to market volatility.

2. Bonds

Bonds are debt securities issued by governments, municipalities, or corporations to raise capital. When investors buy bonds, they are essentially lending money to the issuer in exchange for regular interest payments (coupon payments) and the return of the principal amount at maturity. Bonds are valued for their income-generating potential and relative stability compared to stocks, making them attractive options for conservative investors seeking steady income streams and capital preservation.

3. Mutual Funds

Mutual funds are investment vehicles that pool money from multiple investors to invest in a diversified portfolio of stocks, bonds, or other assets. Managed by professional fund managers, mutual funds offer investors access to a diversified investment portfolio without the need for individual stock or bond selection. Mutual funds are categorized based on their investment objectives, such as growth, income, or balance, and may charge fees known as expense ratios for management and operational expenses.

4. Exchange-traded funds (ETFs)

Exchange-traded funds (ETFs) are similar to mutual funds but trade on stock exchanges like individual stocks. ETFs track various market indices, sectors, or asset classes and offer investors exposure to a broad range of investment opportunities with lower costs and greater liquidity compared to mutual funds. ETFs can be bought and sold throughout the trading day at market prices, providing flexibility and convenience for investors.

5. Real Estate

Real estate investments involve purchasing, owning, and managing physical properties such as residential homes, commercial buildings, or land with the expectation of generating rental income and capital appreciation. Real estate offers diversification benefits and serves as a hedge against inflation, making it an attractive investment option for income-oriented investors seeking stable cash flows and long-term growth potential.

6. Commodities

Commodities are tangible goods or raw materials such as gold, oil, agricultural products, and precious metals that are traded on commodity exchanges. Investors can gain exposure to commodities through various investment vehicles, including futures contracts, exchange-traded funds (ETFs), and mutual funds. Commodities provide diversification benefits and serve as inflation hedges, offering protection against currency devaluation and economic uncertainties.

7. Cryptocurrencies

Cryptocurrencies are digital or virtual currencies that utilize cryptography for security and operate on decentralized networks based on blockchain technology. Popular cryptocurrencies include Bitcoin, Ethereum, and Litecoin, among others. While cryptocurrencies offer the potential for high returns and innovative technologies, they also pose significant risks due to their volatile nature, regulatory uncertainties, and security concerns.

8. Alternative Investments

Alternative investments encompass a wide range of non-traditional assets such as hedge funds, private equity, venture capital, real assets (e.g., infrastructure, timberland), and collectibles (e.g., art, wine). Alternative investments offer diversification benefits and the potential for higher returns but often require higher minimum investments, longer time horizons, and greater due diligence compared to traditional assets.

Investing involves a diverse array of options, each with its own risk-return profile, investment horizon, and liquidity characteristics. By understanding the various types of investments and their underlying features, investors can construct well-balanced investment portfolios tailored to their financial goals, risk tolerance, and time horizon. Whether pursuing growth, income, or capital preservation, diversification across different asset classes is key to mitigating risks and achieving long-term investment success.

6.1 Stocks vs. Bonds vs. Mutual Funds

In the realm of investing, stocks, bonds, and mutual funds represent three distinct asset classes, each offering unique characteristics, risk-return profiles, and investment opportunities. In this section, we delve into the key differences between stocks, bonds, and mutual funds to help investors make informed decisions.

1. Stocks

Definition: Stocks, also known as equities, represent ownership stakes in publicly traded companies. When investors buy stocks, they become shareholders and acquire voting rights and a claim to the company's assets and earnings.

Characteristics:

- **Potential for high returns**: Stocks offer the potential for significant capital appreciation over time, driven by company growth and profitability.
- **Volatility**: Stocks are subject to market fluctuations and can experience significant price swings in response to economic, political, and company-specific factors.
- **Dividends**: Some stocks pay dividends, providing investors with regular income payments in addition to potential capital gains.
- **Voting rights**: Shareholders have the right to vote on company matters, such as the election of the board of directors and major corporate decisions.

2. Bonds

Definition: Bonds are debt securities issued by governments, municipalities, or corporations to raise capital. When investors buy bonds, they are essentially lending money to the issuer in exchange for regular interest payments and the return of the principal amount at maturity.

Characteristics:

- **Fixed income**: Bonds provide a predictable stream of income through regular interest payments (coupon payments) over the bond's term.

- **Capital preservation**: Bonds are generally considered less risky than stocks and offer more predictable returns, making them suitable for conservative investors seeking capital preservation.
- **Maturity date**: Bonds have a specified maturity date, at which point the issuer repays the principal amount to bondholders.
- **Credit risk**: Bonds are subject to credit risk, representing the risk of issuer default or inability to make interest and principal payments.

3. Mutual Funds

Definition: Mutual funds are investment vehicles that pool money from multiple investors to invest in a diversified portfolio of stocks, bonds, or other assets. Managed by professional fund managers, mutual funds offer investors access to a diversified investment portfolio without the need for individual security selection.

Characteristics:

- **Diversification**: Mutual funds invest in a broad range of securities, providing investors with instant diversification and exposure to various asset classes and market sectors.
- **Professional management**: Mutual funds are managed by experienced portfolio managers who make investment decisions based on the fund's stated objectives and investment strategy.
- **Liquidity**: Mutual funds allow investors to buy and sell shares at the fund's net asset value (NAV) at the end of each trading day, providing liquidity and flexibility.

- **Fees**: Mutual funds charge fees known as expense ratios to cover management and operational expenses, which can vary depending on the fund's size and investment strategy.

Comparative Analysis

Risk and Return:

- Stocks typically offer the highest potential for returns but also carry the highest level of risk due to market volatility and company-specific factors.
- Bonds provide a more predictable stream of income and are generally less volatile than stocks, making them suitable for conservative investors seeking stable returns and capital preservation.
- Mutual funds offer diversification benefits and professional management but vary in risk and return depending on the fund's asset allocation and investment strategy.

Income Generation:

- Stocks may provide dividends, but they are not guaranteed and depend on the company's profitability and dividend policy.
- Bonds offer fixed income through regular interest payments, providing investors with a reliable income stream.
- Mutual funds may distribute dividends and interest income generated from the underlying securities to shareholders on a regular basis.

Diversification:

- Stocks represent ownership in individual companies and may lack diversification, exposing investors to company-specific risks.
- Bonds provide diversification benefits but are subject to interest rate risk and credit risk.
- Mutual funds offer instant diversification by investing in a portfolio of securities across different asset classes and market sectors.

Stocks, bonds, and mutual funds represent core components of investment portfolios, each catering to different investor objectives, risk tolerance, and investment horizons. While stocks offer the potential for high returns but higher volatility, bonds provide income generation and capital preservation with lower risk. Mutual funds offer diversification and professional management, making them suitable for investors seeking exposure to a diversified portfolio without the need for individual security selection. By understanding the characteristics and differences between stocks, bonds, and mutual funds, investors can construct well-balanced investment portfolios aligned with their financial goals and risk preferences.

6.2 ETFs and Index Funds

Exchange-Traded Funds (ETFs) and Index Funds are two popular investment vehicles that offer investors exposure to a diversified portfolio of securities while minimizing costs and providing liquidity. In this section, we delve into the key differences and similarities between ETFs and Index Funds to help investors make informed decisions.

1. Exchange-Traded Funds (ETFs)

Definition: ETFs are investment funds that trade on stock exchanges like individual stocks. They typically track a specific index, sector, or asset class and aim to replicate the performance of the underlying benchmark.

Characteristics:

- **Diversification**: ETFs offer instant diversification by holding a portfolio of securities that mirrors the composition of the underlying index or asset class.
- **Liquidity**: ETFs trade on stock exchanges throughout the trading day at market prices, providing investors with flexibility and ease of trading.
- **Transparency**: ETFs disclose their holdings regularly, allowing investors to see the underlying securities and their respective weights in the portfolio.
- **Cost Efficiency**: ETFs generally have lower expense ratios compared to actively managed mutual funds, making them cost-effective investment options.
- **Tax Efficiency**: ETFs are structured in a way that minimizes capital gains distributions, resulting in potentially lower tax liabilities for investors.

2. Index Funds

Definition: Index Funds are mutual funds that aim to replicate the performance of a specific index, such as the S&P 500 or the Dow Jones

Industrial Average. They hold a portfolio of securities that closely mirrors the composition of the underlying index.

Characteristics:

- **Diversification**: Index Funds offer broad diversification by investing in a basket of securities representing the constituents of the underlying index.
- **Professional Management**: Index Funds are typically passively managed, meaning they aim to match the performance of the index rather than outperform it. As a result, they tend to have lower management fees compared to actively managed funds.
- **Cost Efficiency**: Index Funds have lower expense ratios compared to actively managed mutual funds, as they require less research and trading activity.
- **Tax Efficiency**: Index Funds may generate fewer capital gains distributions compared to actively managed funds, resulting in potentially lower tax liabilities for investors.

Comparative Analysis

Structure:

ETFs trade on stock exchanges like individual stocks and can be bought and sold throughout the trading day at market prices. In contrast, Index Funds are mutual funds that are bought and sold at the fund's net asset value (NAV) at the end of each trading day.

Trading Flexibility:

ETFs offer intraday trading flexibility, allowing investors to buy and sell shares at market prices throughout the trading day. Index Funds, on the other hand, can only be bought or sold at the end of the trading day based on the NAV.

Minimum Investments:

ETFs typically have lower minimum investment requirements compared to Index Funds, making them accessible to a broader range of investors.

Expense Ratios:

Both ETFs and Index Funds tend to have lower expense ratios compared to actively managed mutual funds, as they passively track the performance of an index rather than employing active management strategies.

Tax Efficiency:

Both ETFs and Index Funds are tax-efficient investment vehicles, as they tend to generate fewer capital gains distributions compared to actively managed mutual funds.

ETFs and Index Funds are both popular investment vehicles that offer investors exposure to diversified portfolios of securities while minimizing costs and providing liquidity. While ETFs trade on stock exchanges like individual stocks and offer intraday trading flexibility, Index Funds are mutual funds that can only be bought and sold at the end of the trading day based on the NAV. Both ETFs and Index Funds provide diversification, cost efficiency, and tax efficiency, making them attractive options for investors seeking to build well-diversified investment portfolios aligned with their financial goals and risk preferences.

6.3 Diversification Strategies

Diversification is a fundamental principle of investment management aimed at reducing risk by spreading investments across different assets, sectors, and geographical regions. In this section, we explore various diversification strategies that investors can employ to build well-balanced and resilient investment portfolios.

1. Asset Allocation

Asset allocation involves spreading investments across different asset classes, such as stocks, bonds, cash, and alternative investments, based on the investor's financial goals, risk tolerance, and investment horizon. By diversifying across asset classes with low correlation coefficients, investors can reduce portfolio volatility and mitigate the impact of market fluctuations on overall returns.

2. Geographic Diversification

Geographic diversification entails investing in assets across different countries and regions to mitigate country-specific risks, political uncertainties, and economic fluctuations. By allocating investments globally, investors can reduce exposure to domestic market risks and capitalize on growth opportunities in emerging markets while maintaining exposure to established economies.

3. Sector Diversification

Sector diversification involves spreading investments across different industry sectors, such as technology, healthcare, consumer goods, and financial services. By diversifying across sectors, investors can reduce exposure to sector-specific risks and take advantage of opportunities for growth and innovation in diverse segments of the economy.

4. Company Size Diversification

Company size diversification involves investing in companies of different market capitalizations, including large-cap, mid-cap, and small-cap stocks. Large-cap stocks typically offer stability and liquidity, while mid-cap and small-cap stocks may provide higher growth potential but also carry higher volatility. By diversifying across company sizes, investors can balance risk and return potential within their portfolios.

5. Investment Style Diversification

Investment style diversification involves allocating investments across different investment styles, such as value investing, growth investing, and blend investing. Each investment style has unique characteristics and performance drivers, allowing investors to capture opportunities across different market environments and investment cycles.

6. Time Horizon Diversification

Time horizon diversification involves aligning investments with the investor's time horizon, whether short-term, medium-term, or long-term. Short-term investments may focus on liquidity and capital preservation, while long-term investments may prioritize growth and wealth accumulation. By diversifying investments based on time horizon, investors can manage liquidity needs and optimize risk-adjusted returns over time.

7. Alternative Investments

Alternative investments encompass a wide range of non-traditional assets, such as hedge funds, private equity, real estate, and commodities. By allocating a portion of their portfolios to alternative investments, investors can enhance diversification, reduce portfolio volatility, and potentially generate higher returns uncorrelated with traditional asset classes.

8. Risk Management Strategies

Risk management strategies involve implementing hedging techniques, such as options, futures, and derivatives, to protect against downside risks and manage portfolio volatility. By using risk management tools effectively, investors can mitigate losses during market downturns and preserve capital while maximizing returns over the long term.

Diversification is a cornerstone of sound investment management, enabling investors to reduce risk and enhance risk-adjusted returns by spreading investments across different assets, sectors, and strategies. By employing diversification strategies such as asset allocation, geographic diversification, sector diversification, and investment style diversification, investors can build well-balanced and resilient portfolios tailored to their financial goals, risk tolerance, and investment horizon. Additionally, alternative investments and risk management strategies offer additional opportunities for diversification and risk mitigation, allowing investors to navigate the complexities of financial markets with confidence and prudence.

Chapter 7: Building Your Portfolio

Building a portfolio is a critical step in the journey toward achieving financial goals and securing long-term wealth. In this chapter, we delve into the intricacies of portfolio construction, exploring key principles, strategies, and considerations for building a well-balanced and resilient investment portfolio tailored to individual needs and objectives.

Understanding Portfolio Construction

Portfolio construction is the process of assembling a collection of investments that collectively align with an investor's financial goals, risk tolerance, and investment horizon. A well-constructed portfolio aims to optimize risk-adjusted returns by diversifying across different asset classes, sectors, and investment strategies while considering factors such as liquidity, tax efficiency, and cost-effectiveness.

Setting Financial Goals

The first step in building a portfolio is defining clear and achievable financial goals. Whether saving for retirement, funding education expenses, or achieving financial independence, understanding the purpose and time horizon of each goal is essential for determining the appropriate investment strategy and asset allocation.

Assessing Risk Tolerance

Risk tolerance refers to an investor's willingness and ability to withstand fluctuations in the value of their investments. Assessing risk tolerance involves evaluating factors such as investment objectives, time horizon, income needs, and emotional temperament. By understanding their risk tolerance, investors can construct portfolios that balance risk and return in line with their comfort levels.

Asset Allocation

Asset allocation is the process of dividing investments across different asset classes, such as stocks, bonds, cash, and alternative investments, based on their risk-return profiles and correlations. A well-diversified asset allocation strategy aims to optimize risk-adjusted returns while minimizing portfolio volatility and preserving capital over the long term.

Strategic Asset Allocation

Strategic asset allocation involves establishing a target asset allocation based on long-term investment objectives and risk tolerance. It typically involves diversifying investments across a mix of asset classes in proportions that remain relatively constant over time, with periodic rebalancing to maintain the desired allocation.

Tactical Asset Allocation

Tactical asset allocation involves making short-term adjustments to the portfolio's asset allocation based on current market conditions, economic outlook, and investment opportunities. While strategic asset allocation forms the foundation of the portfolio, tactical asset allocation allows investors to capitalize on short-term market inefficiencies and dynamic investment environments.

Investment Selection

Once asset allocation targets are established, investors must select individual investments to populate their portfolios. Factors to consider when selecting investments include:

- **Fundamentals**: Assessing the fundamental characteristics of individual securities, such as financial performance, growth prospects, and valuation metrics.
- **Diversification**: Ensuring a well-diversified portfolio by investing across different asset classes, sectors, and geographic regions to mitigate risk and capture opportunities for growth.
- **Risk Management**: Implementing risk management techniques, such as stop-loss orders, asset allocation, and diversification, to protect against downside risk and preserve capital.
- **Costs and Fees**: Considering the impact of investment costs, including management fees, transaction costs, and taxes, on overall portfolio returns and performance.

Monitoring and Rebalancing

Portfolio monitoring and rebalancing are essential components of effective portfolio management. Regularly monitoring portfolio performance and market conditions allows investors to assess whether their investments remain aligned with their financial goals and risk tolerance. Periodic rebalancing involves realigning the portfolio's asset allocation to the target weights by buying or selling assets as needed to maintain the desired mix.

Building a portfolio is a dynamic and iterative process that requires careful planning, disciplined execution, and ongoing monitoring. By setting clear financial goals, assessing risk tolerance, and establishing a strategic asset allocation, investors can construct well-balanced portfolios that align with their individual needs and objectives. Additionally, selecting high-quality investments, implementing risk management techniques, and regularly monitoring and rebalancing the portfolio is essential for optimizing risk-adjusted returns and achieving long-term investment success. With a sound understanding of portfolio construction principles and strategies, investors can navigate the complexities of financial markets with confidence and prudence, ultimately realizing their financial aspirations and securing a brighter future.

7.1 Choosing Stocks

Selecting individual stocks is a critical aspect of building a well-diversified and high-performing investment portfolio. In this section, we explore key principles, strategies, and considerations for choosing stocks that align with investors' financial goals, risk tolerance, and investment objectives.

Fundamental Analysis

Fundamental analysis involves evaluating the underlying financial health and performance of a company to assess its investment potential. Key factors to consider in fundamental analysis include:

1. Financial Performance

- **Revenue Growth**: Assessing the company's revenue growth over time to gauge its ability to generate top-line growth.
- **Earnings Growth**: Analyzing the company's earnings growth and profitability metrics, such as earnings per share (EPS) and profit margins.
- **Cash Flow**: Evaluating the company's cash flow generation and liquidity position to determine its ability to meet financial obligations and fund future growth initiatives.

2. Business Model and Competitive Advantage

- **Business Model**: Understanding the company's business model, industry dynamics, and competitive positioning to assess its long-term growth prospects and competitive advantage.
- **Moat**: Identifying competitive advantages or economic moats, such as brand recognition, patents, or network effects that provide barriers to entry and protect the company's market share.

3. Management Team

- **Leadership**: Assessing the quality and track record of the company's management team, including their strategic vision, execution capabilities, and alignment with shareholders' interests.
- **Corporate Governance**: Evaluating corporate governance practices, board composition, and transparency to ensure sound stewardship of shareholder capital.

Technical Analysis

Technical analysis involves analyzing historical price and volume data to identify trends, patterns, and trading signals that can inform investment decisions. Key aspects of technical analysis include:

1. Price Trends

- **Trend Analysis**: Identifying the direction and strength of price trends using tools such as moving averages, trendlines, and chart patterns.
- **Support and Resistance Levels**: Identifying key support and resistance levels where buying and selling pressure converge, indicating potential entry and exit points.

2. Momentum Indicators

- **Relative Strength Index (RSI)**: Measuring the speed and change of price movements to assess overbought or oversold conditions.
- **Moving Average Convergence Divergence (MACD)**: Identifying changes in momentum and potential trend reversals based on the relationship between short-term and long-term moving averages.

Valuation Analysis

Valuation analysis involves assessing the intrinsic value of a stock relative to its current market price to determine whether it is overvalued, undervalued, or fairly valued. Key valuation metrics include:

1. Price-to-Earnings (P/E) Ratio

P/E Ratio: Comparing the company's current stock price to its earnings per share (EPS) to assess its valuation relative to its earnings growth potential and industry peers.

2. Price-to-Book (P/B) Ratio

P/B Ratio: Comparing the company's current stock price to its book value per share to assess its valuation relative to its tangible assets and equity position.

3. Dividend Yield

Dividend Yield: Comparing the company's dividend payments to its current stock price to assess its dividend-paying ability and attractiveness to income-oriented investors.

Risk Management

Risk management involves implementing strategies to mitigate downside risk and protect capital in the event of adverse market conditions. Key risk management techniques include:

- **Diversification**: Spreading investments across different stocks, sectors, and asset classes to reduce company-specific and market-related risks.
- **Stop-loss Orders**: Setting predetermined price levels at which to sell stocks to limit potential losses and protect investment capital.
- **Position Sizing**: Determining the appropriate allocation size for each stock position based on risk tolerance and portfolio objectives.

Choosing stocks requires a comprehensive approach that combines fundamental analysis, technical analysis, valuation analysis, and risk management techniques. By conducting thorough research, analyzing financial data, and assessing market trends, investors can identify high-quality stocks with strong growth potential, competitive advantages, and attractive valuations. Additionally, implementing risk management strategies and maintaining a well-diversified portfolio can help investors navigate market volatility and achieve long-term investment success. With disciplined execution and a sound understanding of stock selection principles, investors can build resilient portfolios that withstand market fluctuations and deliver sustainable returns over time.

7.2 Portfolio Allocation Strategies

Portfolio allocation strategies are essential for optimizing risk-adjusted returns and achieving investment objectives. In this section, we explore various portfolio allocation strategies that investors can employ to build well-diversified and resilient investment portfolios tailored to their financial goals, risk tolerance, and investment horizons.

1. Strategic Asset Allocation

Strategic asset allocation involves establishing target allocations to different asset classes based on long-term investment objectives and risk tolerance. Key steps in strategic asset allocation include:

- **Asset Class Selection**: Determining the appropriate mix of asset classes, such as stocks, bonds, cash, and alternative investments, based on their risk-return profiles and correlations.
- **Asset Allocation Targets**: Establishing target allocations to each asset class that align with the investor's financial goals and risk tolerance.
- **Periodic Rebalancing**: Monitoring portfolio performance and rebalancing the asset allocation periodically to maintain the desired mix and manage risk.

2. Tactical Asset Allocation

Tactical asset allocation involves making short-term adjustments to the portfolio's asset allocation based on changing market conditions, economic outlook, and investment opportunities. Key aspects of tactical asset allocation include:

- **Market Analysis**: Analyzing macroeconomic trends, market valuations, and geopolitical developments to identify potential opportunities and risks.
- **Asset Class Rotation**: Adjusting portfolio allocations to overweight or underweight certain asset classes based on their relative attractiveness and expected performance.
- **Active Management**: Actively managing the portfolio to capitalize on short-term market inefficiencies and dynamic investment environments while staying aligned with long-term investment objectives.

3. Risk Parity Allocation

Risk parity allocation aims to equalize the risk contribution of each asset class within the portfolio, rather than relying solely on market capitalization or asset allocation targets. Key principles of risk parity allocation include:

- **Risk Budgeting**: Allocating risk budgets to different asset classes based on their historical volatilities and correlations to achieve a balanced risk exposure.

- **Diversification**: Spreading risk across multiple asset classes with low correlations to reduce portfolio volatility and enhance risk-adjusted returns.
- **Dynamic Rebalancing**: Adjusting portfolio allocations dynamically to maintain risk parity and adapt to changing market conditions and risk factors.

4. Factor-Based Allocation

Factor-based allocation involves tilting portfolio allocations towards specific investment factors, such as value, growth, momentum, and quality, to capture excess returns and enhance portfolio performance. Key aspects of factor-based allocation include:

- **Factor Selection**: Identifying investment factors that have historically generated excess returns and exhibit persistent performance over time.
- **Factor Exposure**: Tilting portfolio allocations towards factors that are expected to outperform based on market conditions, economic trends, and valuation metrics.
- **Factor Diversification**: Diversifying factor exposures across multiple dimensions to reduce concentration risk and enhance risk-adjusted returns.

5. Goals-Based Allocation

Goals-based allocation involves structuring portfolio allocations around specific financial goals and liabilities, such as retirement planning, education funding, and wealth preservation. Key elements of goals-based allocation include:

- **Goal Identification**: Identifying and prioritizing financial goals based on their importance, time horizon, and funding requirements.
- **Liability Matching**: Allocating assets to match the timing and cash flow needs of each financial goal, taking into account factors such as inflation, taxes, and market volatility.
- **Dynamic Adjustments**: Adjusting portfolio allocations over time to reflect changes in financial goals, market conditions, and life circumstances while staying focused on achieving long-term objectives.

Portfolio allocation strategies play a critical role in determining investment outcomes and achieving financial success. By employing strategic asset allocation, tactical asset allocation, risk parity allocation, factor-based allocation, or goals-based allocation, investors can build well-diversified portfolios that align with their financial goals, risk tolerance, and investment horizons. Additionally, regular monitoring and rebalancing of portfolio allocations are essential for maintaining alignment with investment objectives and managing risk effectively. With a disciplined approach to portfolio allocation and a sound understanding of investment principles, investors can navigate the complexities of financial markets and achieve long-term investment success.

7.3 Rebalancing and Monitoring

Rebalancing and monitoring are critical aspects of effective portfolio management, ensuring that investment portfolios remain aligned with investors' financial goals, risk tolerance, and investment objectives. In this section, we explore the importance of rebalancing and monitoring and provide guidelines for implementing these practices effectively.

Rebalancing

Rebalancing involves adjusting portfolio allocations to maintain the desired asset mix and risk exposure over time. The primary objectives of rebalancing are to:

- **Restore Asset Allocation**: Bring portfolio allocations back to target levels to ensure consistency with long-term investment objectives and risk tolerance.
- **Manage Risk**: Mitigate portfolio drift and reduce exposure to overvalued or underperforming asset classes, sectors, or securities.
- **Capture Opportunities**: Take advantage of market inefficiencies and asset class rotations to enhance portfolio performance and capitalize on investment opportunities.

Rebalancing Strategies:

Time-Based Rebalancing: Set predetermined time intervals, such as quarterly, semi-annually, or annually, to review portfolio allocations and rebalance as needed.

- **Threshold-Based Rebalancing**: Monitor deviations from target allocations and rebalance when portfolio allocations drift beyond predefined thresholds, such as ±5% from target levels.
- **Calendar-Based Rebalancing**: Rebalance portfolios at specific calendar dates, such as the end of the year or fiscal quarter, to maintain alignment with investment objectives and market conditions.

Monitoring

Monitoring involves regularly assessing portfolio performance, market conditions, and economic trends to ensure that investment strategies remain effective and aligned with investors' objectives. Key elements of portfolio monitoring include:

- **Performance Review**: Evaluate portfolio returns, volatility, and risk-adjusted metrics relative to benchmarks and investment objectives.
- **Market Analysis**: Analyze macroeconomic indicators, sector trends, and geopolitical developments to identify potential opportunities and risks.
- **Risk Assessment**: Assess portfolio risk factors, such as volatility, correlation, and downside potential, to identify areas of vulnerability and implement risk management strategies.
- **Fundamental Analysis**: Review the underlying fundamentals of individual securities, sectors, and asset classes to assess valuation, growth prospects, and competitive positioning.

Monitoring Practices:

- **Regular Reviews**: Conduct periodic portfolio reviews, such as monthly or quarterly, to assess performance, review market conditions, and adjust investment strategies as needed.
- **Benchmark Comparison**: Compare portfolio performance against relevant benchmarks, indices, or peer groups to evaluate relative performance and identify areas for improvement.
- **Scenario Analysis**: Conduct scenario analysis and stress testing to assess the impact of potential market events, economic shocks, and adverse scenarios on portfolio performance and risk exposure.

Implementation Guidelines

- **Discipline**: Maintain discipline and consistency in implementing rebalancing and monitoring practices, adhering to predetermined guidelines and objectives.
- **Flexibility**: Remain flexible and adaptive in response to changing market conditions, economic trends, and investment opportunities, adjusting portfolio allocations and strategies as needed.
- **Documentation**: Keep detailed records of rebalancing decisions, monitoring activities, and portfolio performance metrics to track progress, evaluate effectiveness, and inform future decisions.

Rebalancing and monitoring are essential components of effective portfolio management, enabling investors to maintain alignment with their financial goals, risk tolerance, and investment objectives over time. By implementing disciplined rebalancing strategies and conducting regular portfolio reviews and monitoring activities, investors can manage risk, capture opportunities, and achieve long-term investment success. With a proactive approach to portfolio management and a commitment to ongoing monitoring and evaluation, investors can navigate the complexities of financial markets with confidence and prudence, ultimately realizing their financial aspirations and securing a brighter future.

Chapter 8: Strategies for Success

Success in investing requires a combination of discipline, knowledge, and strategic decision-making. In this chapter, we explore key strategies and principles that can help investors achieve their financial goals, build wealth, and navigate the complexities of financial markets with confidence and prudence.

1. Goal Setting

Setting clear and achievable financial goals is the first step towards investment success. Whether saving for retirement, funding education expenses, or achieving financial independence, defining specific goals provides direction and motivation for building a well-structured investment portfolio.

2. Risk Management

Effective risk management is essential for protecting capital and preserving wealth over the long term. Key risk management strategies include diversification, asset allocation, and the use of risk mitigation techniques such as stop-loss orders and hedging strategies.

3. Discipline and Patience

Maintaining discipline and patience is crucial in navigating the ups and downs of financial markets. Avoiding impulsive decisions driven by emotions and sticking to a well-defined investment plan can help investors stay focused on their long-term objectives and avoid costly mistakes.

4. Education and Continuous Learning

Investing is a dynamic and evolving field, and staying informed about market trends, economic developments, and investment strategies is essential for success. Continuously educating oneself through books, courses, and seminars can enhance investment knowledge and decision-making skills.

5. Asset Allocation

Strategic asset allocation involves spreading investments across different asset classes to optimize risk-adjusted returns. By diversifying across stocks, bonds, cash, and alternative investments, investors can mitigate risk and capture opportunities for growth in various market conditions.

6. Active vs. Passive Investing

Choosing between active and passive investing approaches depends on individual preferences, investment objectives, and risk tolerance. While active investing involves actively selecting and managing individual securities to outperform the market, passive investing focuses on tracking market indices through low-cost index funds or exchange-traded funds (ETFs).

7. Long-Term Perspective

Adopting a long-term investment perspective can help investor's weather short-term market volatility and achieve sustainable returns over time. By focusing on fundamental principles, staying patient during market fluctuations, and maintaining a diversified portfolio, investors can capture the benefits of long-term compounding and wealth accumulation.

8. Regular Monitoring and Rebalancing

Regularly monitoring portfolio performance and rebalancing asset allocations ensures that investments remain aligned with financial goals and risk tolerance. By periodically reviewing portfolio allocations, adjusting positions, and staying attuned to changing market conditions, investors can optimize risk-adjusted returns and adapt to evolving investment landscapes.

Success in investing requires a combination of strategic planning, disciplined execution, and continuous learning. By setting clear financial goals, managing risk effectively, staying disciplined and patient, and maintaining a long-term perspective, investors can navigate financial markets with confidence and prudence, ultimately achieving their financial aspirations and securing a brighter future for themselves and their families. With a commitment to ongoing education, diligent portfolio management, and sound investment principles, investors can embark on a journey toward long-term financial success and prosperity.

8.1 Long-Term vs. Short-Term Investing

Investing strategies can vary widely based on the time horizon of the investor. In this section, we explore the differences between long-term and short-term investing, along with their respective advantages, considerations, and implications for investors.

Long-Term Investing

Long-term investing involves holding assets for an extended period, typically years or decades, with the goal of achieving capital appreciation and wealth accumulation over time. Key characteristics of long-term investing include:

- **Time Horizon**: Long-term investors focus on the big picture and are willing to ride out short-term market fluctuations to realize their investment objectives.
- **Compound Growth**: Long-term investing harnesses the power of compounding, where investment returns are reinvested to generate additional returns over time, leading to exponential growth.
- **Risk Management**: Long-term investors prioritize risk management and diversification, recognizing that short-term market volatility is often outweighed by the potential for long-term growth.

Advantages:

- **Compounding**: Long-term investors benefit from the compounding effect, where reinvested returns generate additional returns, accelerating wealth accumulation over time.
- **Reduced Trading Costs**: Long-term investing typically involves fewer transactions, leading to lower brokerage fees, taxes, and other trading costs compared to frequent trading.
- **Tax Efficiency**: Long-term capital gains are taxed at lower rates than short-term capital gains, providing tax advantages for investors who hold assets for an extended period.

Short-Term Investing

Short-term investing involves buying and selling assets within a relatively short time frame, typically days, weeks, or months, with the goal of capitalizing on short-term market movements and price fluctuations. Key characteristics of short-term investing include:

- **Market Timing**: Short-term investors attempt to profit from short-term price movements and market trends, often using technical analysis and trading strategies to time their trades.
- **Liquidity**: Short-term investors prioritize liquidity and flexibility, actively buying and selling assets to capitalize on short-term trading opportunities and market inefficiencies.
- **Risk Exposure**: Short-term investing carries higher risks due to increased market volatility, shorter holding periods, and the potential for losses from mistimed trades.

Advantages:

- **Profit Potential**: Short-term investors have the potential to generate quick profits by capitalizing on short-term market movements and trading opportunities.
- **Flexibility**: Short-term investing provides flexibility to adapt to changing market conditions and capitalize on emerging trends and opportunities.
- **Hedging Strategies**: Short-term investors can use derivatives, options, and other hedging strategies to protect against downside risk and manage portfolio volatility.

Considerations

- **Risk Tolerance**: Long-term investing is generally more suitable for investors with a higher risk tolerance and longer investment horizon, while short-term investing may be better suited for investors with a higher tolerance for risk and volatility.
- **Investment Objectives**: Long-term investing is ideal for achieving long-term financial goals such as retirement planning, wealth accumulation, and legacy planning, while short-term investing may be more suitable for generating supplemental income or capitalizing on market opportunities.
- **Market Conditions**: Market conditions, economic outlook, and investor sentiment can influence the suitability of long-term vs. short-term investing strategies, with each approach offering unique advantages and challenges in different market environments.

Both long-term and short-term investing strategies have their merits and considerations, depending on investors' financial goals, risk tolerance, and investment objectives. Long-term investing offers the potential for compounding growth, reduced trading costs, and tax advantages, while short-term investing provides opportunities for quick profits, flexibility, and hedging strategies. By understanding the differences between long-term and short-term investing and aligning investment strategies with individual preferences and circumstances, investors can optimize risk-adjusted returns and achieve long-term investment success.

8.2 Dollar-Cost Averaging

Dollar-cost averaging (DCA) is an investment strategy that involves regularly investing a fixed amount of money into a particular asset or investment vehicle over time, regardless of market conditions. In this section, we explore the concept of dollar-cost averaging, its benefits, and considerations for investors.

How Dollar-Cost Averaging Works

Dollar-cost averaging works by spreading investment purchases over time, rather than investing a lump sum of money all at once. Investors commit to investing a fixed dollar amount at regular intervals, such as weekly, monthly, or quarterly, regardless of whether the market is up or down. This approach allows investors to purchase more shares when prices are low and fewer shares when prices are high, ultimately averaging out the cost of acquiring assets over time.

Benefits of Dollar-Cost Averaging

1. Risk Mitigation

Dollar-cost averaging helps mitigate the impact of market volatility on investment returns. By investing consistently over time, investors avoid the risk of making large investments at market peaks and minimize the impact of short-term price fluctuations on their overall portfolio performance.

2. Disciplined Investing

Dollar-cost averaging encourages disciplined investing behavior by automating the investment process and removing the temptation to time the market. By committing to regular investment contributions, investors establish a consistent savings habit and stay focused on their long-term financial goals.

3. Potential for Lower Average Cost

Dollar-cost averaging has the potential to lower the average cost per share of an investment over time. By purchasing more shares when prices are low and fewer shares when prices are high, investors can achieve a lower average cost basis for their holdings, enhancing long-term returns when prices eventually rise.

4. Psychological Benefits

Dollar-cost averaging can provide psychological benefits by reducing the stress and anxiety associated with market timing and short-term fluctuations. By adopting a systematic investment approach, investors can avoid emotional decision-making and stay committed to their long-term investment strategy.

Considerations for Investors

1. Time Horizon

Dollar-cost averaging works best for investors with a long-term investment horizon. While it can help mitigate short-term market volatility, it may not be suitable for investors with immediate liquidity needs or short-term investment objectives.

2. Investment Selection

Investors should carefully consider the selection of assets or investment vehicles for dollar-cost averaging. Diversifying across different asset classes and sectors can help manage risk and optimize long-term returns.

3. Cost Considerations

Investors should be mindful of transaction costs, such as brokerage fees or mutual fund expenses when implementing a dollar-cost averaging strategy. Choosing low-cost investment options can help maximize the benefits of regular investing over time.

4. Monitoring and Review

While dollar-cost averaging is a passive investment strategy, investors should periodically review their investment portfolios and adjust their contributions as needed based on changes in financial circumstances, market conditions, and investment objectives.

Dollar-cost averaging is a simple yet effective investment strategy that can help investors build wealth over time by consistently investing a fixed amount of money at regular intervals. By mitigating the impact of market volatility, encouraging disciplined investing behavior, and potentially lowering the average cost per share of investments, dollar-cost averaging offers a practical approach to achieving long-term financial goals. With careful planning, prudent investment selection, and disciplined execution, investors can harness the power of dollar-cost averaging to build resilient investment portfolios and secure a brighter financial future.

8.3 Managing Emotions and Risk

Emotions and risk are inherent aspects of investing that can significantly impact investment decisions and outcomes. In this section, we explore strategies for managing emotions and risk effectively to make informed and rational investment decisions.

Understanding Emotions in Investing

Emotions such as fear, greed, and euphoria can cloud judgment and lead investors to make irrational decisions. Common emotional pitfalls in investing include:

- **Fear of Missing Out (FOMO)**: The fear of missing out on potential gains can lead investors to chase hot investment trends or assets, often at inflated prices.
- **Loss Aversion**: The tendency to prioritize avoiding losses over realizing gains can cause investors to sell winning investments prematurely or hold onto losing investments for too long.
- **Overconfidence**: Excessive confidence in one's ability to predict market movements or pick winning investments can lead to overtrading, excessive risk-taking, and poor investment performance.

Strategies for Managing Emotions

1. Establish Clear Investment Objectives

Setting clear and achievable investment objectives helps investors stay focused on their long-term financial goals and avoid making impulsive decisions driven by short-term market fluctuations or emotional impulses.

2. Develop a Written Investment Plan

Creating a written investment plan with predefined asset allocation targets, risk tolerance levels, and rebalancing guidelines provides a structured framework for making investment decisions and helps investors stay disciplined during periods of market volatility.

3. Practice Patience and Discipline

Maintaining patience and discipline is essential in navigating the ups and downs of financial markets. Avoid making knee-jerk reactions to short-term market movements and stick to your investment plan, even during periods of uncertainty or market turbulence.

4. Conduct Thorough Research

Thorough research and due diligence can help investors make informed and rational investment decisions based on fundamental analysis, market trends, and economic indicators. By understanding the underlying factors driving investment opportunities, investors can make more confident and reasoned investment choices.

Understanding and Managing Risk

Risk is an inherent aspect of investing that encompasses various factors, including market risk, credit risk, liquidity risk, and behavioral risk. Key principles for managing risk include:

- **Diversification**: Spreading investments across different asset classes, sectors, and geographic regions can help reduce portfolio volatility and mitigate the impact of adverse market events.
- **Asset Allocation**: Establishing a strategic asset allocation that aligns with investment objectives and risk tolerance can help optimize risk-adjusted returns and manage portfolio risk effectively.
- **Risk Assessment**: Regularly assessing portfolio risk factors, monitoring market conditions, and stress-testing investment portfolios can help identify potential risks and vulnerabilities and implement appropriate risk management strategies.

Managing emotions and risk is essential for making informed and rational investment decisions and achieving long-term investment success. By understanding common emotional pitfalls in investing, developing strategies for managing emotions effectively, and implementing sound risk management practices, investors can navigate financial markets with confidence and prudence, ultimately realizing their financial goals and securing a brighter future. With patience, discipline, and a commitment to ongoing education and self-awareness, investors can overcome emotional biases, mitigate portfolio risk, and achieve sustainable investment outcomes over time.

Chapter 9: Tools and Resources

In today's digital age, investors have access to a vast array of tools and resources to support their investment decisions and portfolio management efforts. In this chapter, we explore some of the most valuable tools and resources available to investors, ranging from market research platforms to investment calculators and educational resources.

1. Financial News and Analysis Platforms

Financial news and analysis platforms provide investors with real-time market news, commentary, and analysis from leading financial experts and analysts. Popular platforms include Bloomberg, CNBC, Reuters, and MarketWatch, which offer comprehensive coverage of global financial markets, economic trends, and investment insights.

2. Investment Research Websites

Investment research websites offer in-depth analysis, research reports, and stock recommendations to help investors make informed investment decisions. Websites such as Morningstar, Seeking Alpha, and Zacks Investment Research provide access to company profiles, financial data, and expert analysis to support investment research and due diligence.

3. Online Brokerage Platforms

Online brokerage platforms enable investors to buy and sell securities, manage their investment portfolios, and access a wide range of investment products and services. Leading online brokerages such as Charles Schwab, Fidelity, TD Ameritrade, and Robinhood offer user-friendly interfaces, competitive pricing, and a variety of trading tools and research resources.

4. Investment Apps

Investment apps provide investors with convenient access to their investment portfolios, market news, and trading capabilities on mobile devices. Popular investment apps include Robinhood, Acorns, and Stash, which offer commission-free trading, automated investing, and educational resources to help users build wealth and achieve their financial goals.

5. Investment Calculators

Investment calculators help investors analyze various financial scenarios, estimate investment returns, and plan for future financial goals. Common types of investment calculators include retirement calculators, savings calculators, and investment return calculators, which enable users to assess the impact of different investment strategies and scenarios on their long-term financial well-being.

6. Educational Resources

Educational resources play a crucial role in helping investors improve their investment knowledge and decision-making skills. Online courses, webinars, and educational websites such as Investopedia, Khan Academy, and Coursera offer a wealth of educational content on topics such as investing basics, financial planning, and advanced investment strategies.

7. Financial Planning Software

Financial planning software provides investors with tools and resources to create and manage comprehensive financial plans, track expenses, and monitor progress toward financial goals. Platforms such as Personal Capital, Mint, and Quicken offer budgeting tools, investment tracking, and retirement planning features to help users achieve financial security and independence.

Tools and resources play a vital role in supporting investors' investment decisions, portfolio management efforts, and financial planning activities. By leveraging financial news platforms, investment research websites, online brokerage platforms, investment apps, investment calculators, educational resources, and financial planning software, investors can access valuable information, analysis, and tools to help them make informed decisions, build diversified portfolios, and achieve their long-term financial goals. With a commitment to ongoing education, research, and prudent decision-making, investors can navigate financial markets with confidence and achieve sustainable investment success over time.

9.1 Online Brokerages

Online brokerages have revolutionized the way investors buy and sell securities, offering convenient access to financial markets, competitive pricing, and a wide range of investment products and services. In this section, we explore the features, benefits, and considerations of online brokerages for investors.

Features of Online Brokerages

1. Trading Platform

Online brokerages provide user-friendly trading platforms that enable investors to execute trades, monitor market activity, and access real-time quotes and charts. These platforms offer intuitive interfaces, advanced trading tools, and customizable features to meet the needs of both novice and experienced investors.

2. Investment Products

Online brokerages offer access to a diverse range of investment products, including stocks, bonds, mutual funds, exchange-traded funds (ETFs), options, futures, and foreign exchange (forex) instruments. Investors can build diversified portfolios tailored to their risk tolerance, investment objectives, and financial goals.

3. Research and Analysis

Many online brokerages provide research and analysis tools to help investors make informed investment decisions. These tools may include market news, analyst reports, financial data, screening tools, and charting capabilities, empowering investors to conduct thorough research and due diligence on potential investment opportunities.

4. Educational Resources

Online brokerages often offer educational resources and tutorials to help investors learn about investing basics, trading strategies, and financial markets. These resources may include articles, videos, webinars, and online courses designed to improve investors' knowledge and confidence in managing their investment portfolios.

5. Customer Support

Online brokerages typically offer customer support services to assist investors with account setup, trading inquiries, technical issues, and general assistance. Customer support may be available via phone, email, live chat, or in-person consultations, depending on the brokerage's policies and resources.

Benefits of Online Brokerages

1. Accessibility

Online brokerages offer convenient access to financial markets, allowing investors to trade securities anytime, anywhere, using desktop computers, laptops, tablets, or mobile devices. This accessibility enables investors to react quickly to market developments and capitalize on investment opportunities in real time.

2. Cost-Efficiency

Online brokerages often feature competitive pricing structures with lower commissions, fees, and minimum account requirements compared to traditional full-service brokerages. This cost-efficiency allows investors to save money on trading expenses and retain more of their investment returns over time.

3. Transparency

Online brokerages provide transparency in pricing, execution, and order handling, allowing investors to see real-time quotes, market data, and trade confirmations. This transparency fosters trust and confidence in the brokerage's operations and helps investors make informed decisions about their investments.

4. Control

Online brokerages empower investors to take control of their investment portfolios and trading decisions, without relying on intermediaries or financial advisors. Investors have the flexibility to research, analyze, and execute trades independently, tailoring their investment strategies to their individual preferences and objectives.

Considerations for Investors

1. Trading Costs

While online brokerages typically offer lower commissions and fees than traditional brokerages, investors should be mindful of trading costs, including commissions, spreads, and other transaction fees, which can impact investment returns, especially for frequent traders or investors with large portfolios.

2. Platform Reliability

Investors should evaluate the reliability and performance of online trading platforms, including uptime, speed, and stability, to ensure smooth and efficient execution of trades, especially during periods of high market volatility or heavy trading activity.

3. Security and Privacy

Investors should prioritize security and privacy when choosing an online brokerage, ensuring that the brokerage employs robust security measures, such as encryption, multi-factor authentication, and secure data storage, to protect clients' personal and financial information from unauthorized access or cyber threats.

Online brokerages offer investors a convenient, cost-effective, and transparent way to access financial markets, trade securities, and manage investment portfolios. With user-friendly trading platforms, diverse investment products, research and analysis tools, educational resources, and responsive customer support, online brokerages empower investors to take control of their financial futures and achieve their long-term investment goals. By carefully evaluating the features, benefits, and considerations of online brokerages, investors can select the platform that best meets their needs and preferences, positioning themselves for success in the dynamic and ever-evolving world of investing.

9.2 Research Platforms

Research platforms play a vital role in helping investors make informed decisions by providing access to a wealth of information, analysis, and tools related to financial markets and investment opportunities. In this section, we explore the features, benefits, and considerations of research platforms for investors.

Features of Research Platforms

1. Market News and Analysis

Research platforms offer real-time market news, commentary, and analysis from leading financial experts and analysts. These platforms provide insights into market trends, economic indicators, and geopolitical developments, helping investors stay informed about key drivers of market movements and investment opportunities.

2. Company Research and Analysis

Research platforms provide access to in-depth research reports, company profiles, and financial data for individual companies. Investors can analyze fundamental metrics, such as earnings growth, revenue trends, and valuation multiples, to evaluate investment opportunities and make informed decisions about buying or selling stocks.

3. Sector and Industry Analysis

Research platforms offer sector and industry analysis to help investors identify emerging trends, growth opportunities, and potential risks within specific sectors of the economy. By understanding sector dynamics and industry fundamentals, investors can allocate capital strategically and position their portfolios for long-term growth and outperformance.

4. Technical Analysis Tools

Research platforms provide technical analysis tools and charting capabilities to help investors analyze price movements, identify patterns, and make informed trading decisions. These tools may include moving averages, trend lines, oscillators, and other technical indicators that enable investors to assess market sentiment and anticipate price trends.

5. Screening and Filtering

Research platforms offer screening and filtering tools to help investors identify investment opportunities based on specific criteria, such as market capitalization, industry sector, valuation metrics, and growth prospects. These tools allow investors to narrow down their search and focus on securities that meet their investment criteria and objectives.

Benefits of Research Platforms

1. Information Access

Research platforms provide investors with access to a vast array of information, analysis, and data sources, enabling them to conduct thorough research and due diligence on potential investment opportunities. By staying informed about market trends and company fundamentals, investors can make more confident and informed investment decisions.

2. Decision Support

Research platforms offer decision support tools and resources to help investors evaluate investment opportunities, assess risks, and construct well-informed investment portfolios. Whether analyzing individual stocks, sectors, or asset classes, investors can leverage research platforms to enhance their decision-making process and optimize investment outcomes.

3. Education and Insights

Research platforms provide educational resources, market insights, and expert commentary to help investors expand their investment knowledge and improve their understanding of financial markets. By learning from industry experts and staying abreast of market developments, investors can enhance their investment skills and become more effective and successful investors over time.

Considerations for Investors

1. Data Quality and Reliability

Investors should evaluate the quality and reliability of data and analysis provided by research platforms, ensuring that information is accurate, up-to-date, and sourced from reputable sources. Verifying the credibility and integrity of data sources can help investors make more informed and reliable investment decisions.

2. Platform Usability and Functionality

Investors should assess the usability and functionality of research platforms, including user interface design, navigation tools, and search capabilities. A user-friendly platform with intuitive features and customizable settings can enhance the user experience and facilitate efficient research and analysis.

3. Cost and Accessibility

Investors should consider the cost and accessibility of research platforms, including subscription fees, membership requirements, and access restrictions. Evaluating the value proposition and cost-benefit trade-offs of research platforms can help investors determine whether the platform aligns with their investment needs and preferences.

Research platforms provide investors with valuable tools and resources to conduct thorough research, analyze investment opportunities, and make informed decisions in financial markets. By accessing market news and analysis, company research, sector insights, technical analysis tools, and screening capabilities, investors can enhance their investment knowledge, improve their decision-making process, and achieve their long-term financial goals. With a commitment to ongoing education, research, and prudent decision-making, investors can leverage research platforms to navigate financial markets with confidence and achieve sustainable investment success over time.

9.3 Investment Apps

Investment apps have become increasingly popular among investors, offering convenient access to financial markets, intuitive trading platforms, and a wide range of investment products and services. In this section, we explore the features, benefits, and considerations of investment apps for investors.

Features of Investment Apps

1. User-Friendly Interface

Investment apps feature user-friendly interfaces designed for ease of use and accessibility, allowing investors to navigate the platform, execute trades, and access investment information with ease. Intuitive design elements, such as customizable dashboards and simplified trading workflows, enhance the user experience and facilitate efficient investing.

2. Mobile Trading

Investment apps enable investors to trade securities, manage investment portfolios, and monitor market activity on-the-go, using smartphones or tablets. Mobile trading features real-time market data, order execution capabilities, and account management tools, empowering investors to stay connected to financial markets and make informed investment decisions from anywhere, at any time.

3. Commission-Free Trading

Many investment apps offer commission-free trading, allowing investors to buy and sell stocks, ETFs, and other securities without paying traditional brokerage commissions or transaction fees. This cost-effective pricing model enables investors to save money on trading expenses and retain more of their investment returns over time.

4. Fractional Shares

Some investment apps offer fractional share investing, allowing investors to purchase partial shares of expensive stocks or ETFs for as little as $1. This feature enables investors to diversify their portfolios, access high-priced securities, and invest smaller amounts of capital, regardless of share price.

5. Educational Resources

Investment apps provide educational resources, tutorials, and research tools to help investors improve their investment knowledge and decision-making skills. These resources may include articles, videos, webinars, and interactive learning modules covering topics such as investing basics, market trends, and portfolio management strategies.

Benefits of Investment Apps

1. Accessibility

Investment apps offer convenient access to financial markets and investment opportunities, allowing investors to trade securities, manage portfolios, and access investment information anytime, anywhere, using mobile devices. This accessibility enables investors to react quickly to market developments and capitalize on investment opportunities in real-time.

2. Cost-Efficiency

Investment apps often feature low-cost pricing structures with commission-free trading and competitive fees, making investing more accessible and affordable for investors of all levels. By eliminating traditional brokerage commissions and transaction fees, investment apps help investors save money on trading expenses and maximize their investment returns over time.

3. Flexibility

Investment apps provide investors with the flexibility to tailor their investment strategies to their individual preferences, risk tolerance, and financial goals. Whether investing in stocks, ETFs, mutual funds, or other securities, investors can customize their portfolios, adjust allocations, and execute trades according to their specific investment objectives and preferences.

Considerations for Investors

1. Platform Security

Investors should prioritize platform security when choosing an investment app, ensuring that the app employs robust security measures, such as encryption, multi-factor authentication, and secure data storage, to protect users' personal and financial information from unauthorized access or cyber threats.

2. Account Fees and Charges

While many investment apps offer commission-free trading, investors should be aware of other account fees and charges, such as account maintenance fees, margin interest, and foreign exchange fees, which can impact overall investment returns, especially for frequent traders or investors with large portfolios.

3. Platform Reliability

Investors should evaluate the reliability and performance of investment apps, including uptime, speed, and stability, to ensure smooth and efficient execution of trades and account management tasks. A reliable platform with minimal downtime and responsive customer support can enhance the user experience and instill confidence in the app's operations.

Investment apps offer investors a convenient, cost-effective, and flexible way to access financial markets, trade securities, and manage investment portfolios on-the-go. With user-friendly interfaces, commission-free trading, fractional share investing, educational resources, and intuitive mobile trading features, investment apps empower investors to take control of their financial futures and achieve their long-term investment goals. By carefully evaluating the features, benefits, and considerations of investment apps, investors can select the app that best meets their needs and preferences, positioning themselves for success in the dynamic and ever-evolving world of investing.

Chapter 10: Common Mistakes to Avoid

Investing can be a rewarding journey, but it's not without its pitfalls. In this chapter, we delve into some of the most common mistakes that investors make and offer insights on how to avoid them, helping you navigate the world of investing with greater confidence and success.

1. Lack of Research and Due Diligence

One of the most common mistakes investors make is diving into investments without conducting thorough research and due diligence. Failing to understand the fundamentals of an investment, such as the company's financial health, competitive position, and growth prospects, can lead to poor investment decisions and unnecessary risk.

2. Emotional Investing

Emotions can cloud judgment and lead investors to make impulsive decisions based on fear, greed, or overconfidence. Emotional investing often results in buying high and selling low, as investors react to short-term market fluctuations instead of sticking to a long-term investment strategy. Avoiding emotional decision-making and staying disciplined in the face of market volatility is essential for long-term investment success.

3. Lack of Diversification

Putting all your eggs in one basket is a common mistake that can expose investors to unnecessary risk. Failing to diversify across different asset classes, sectors, and geographic regions can leave investors vulnerable to concentrated risks and market downturns. Building a well-diversified portfolio helps spread risk and mitigate the impact of adverse events on investment returns.

4. Trying to Time the Market

Attempting to time the market by predicting short-term price movements is a risky strategy that often leads to disappointment. Market timing is notoriously difficult, and even seasoned investors struggle to consistently outperform the market through timing alone. Instead of trying to time the market, focus on long-term investing principles, such as asset allocation, diversification, and disciplined investing.

5. Chasing Hot Tips and Trends

Following hot tips and chasing investment trends can be tempting, but it's rarely a recipe for success. By the time investment becomes a hot tip or a popular trend, much of its potential upside may already be priced in, leaving latecomers exposed to downside risk. Instead of chasing the latest fad, focus on fundamental analysis, research, and investing in companies with strong fundamentals and long-term growth potential.

6. Neglecting Risk Management

Ignoring risk management principles is a common mistake that can have devastating consequences for investors. Failing to assess and mitigate risks, such as market risk, credit risk, and liquidity risk, can expose investors to significant losses during market downturns or unexpected events. Implementing risk management strategies, such as diversification, asset allocation, and stop-loss orders, is essential for protecting capital and preserving wealth over the long term.

Avoiding common investment mistakes is crucial for achieving long-term investment success and building wealth over time. By conducting thorough research and due diligence, staying disciplined in the face of market volatility, diversifying across asset classes, avoiding market timing traps, resisting the urge to chase hot tips, and implementing robust risk management practices, investors can navigate the complexities of financial markets with greater confidence and resilience. With a commitment to learning from mistakes and continuously improving investment strategies, investors can enhance their financial well-being and achieve their long-term investment goals.

10.1 Chasing Hot Stocks

Chasing hot stocks is a common mistake that investors often make, driven by the allure of quick profits and the fear of missing out on lucrative investment opportunities. In this section, we explore the dangers of chasing hot stocks and offer insights on how to avoid this common investment trap.

Understanding the Temptation

Chasing hot stocks occurs when investors rush to buy shares of companies that have recently experienced rapid price appreciation or gained significant media attention. These stocks are often fueled by market speculation, hype, or positive news catalysts, enticing investors with the promise of high returns in a short period.

The Risks Involved

While the allure of hot stocks may seem irresistible, chasing them can lead to several risks and pitfalls:

1. Overvaluation

Hot stocks often become overvalued as investors bid up prices based on speculative expectations rather than underlying fundamentals. Buying overvalued stocks increases the risk of capital loss if prices eventually revert to more reasonable levels.

2. Market Volatility

Hot stocks are susceptible to significant price swings and heightened volatility, making them inherently risky investments. Rapid price movements can result in sudden losses, particularly for investors who enter positions at peak valuations.

3. Herd Mentality

Chasing hot stocks often involves following the herd mentality, where investors buy into a stock simply because others are doing so, without conducting proper research or analysis. Herd behavior can amplify market bubbles and lead to sharp corrections when sentiment shifts.

How to Avoid the Trap

Avoiding the temptation to chase hot stocks requires discipline, patience, and a focus on long-term investment principles:

1. Conduct Thorough Research

Instead of chasing the latest market craze, focus on companies with strong fundamentals, sound business models, and sustainable growth prospects. Conduct thorough research and due diligence to assess the intrinsic value of a stock before considering an investment.

2. Stick to Your Investment Strategy

Develop a well-defined investment strategy based on your financial goals, risk tolerance, and time horizon. Stay disciplined and avoid deviating from your strategy in response to short-term market fluctuations or hype surrounding hot stocks.

3. Diversify Your Portfolio

Diversification is key to managing risk and reducing exposure to individual stock volatility. Spread your investments across different asset classes, sectors, and geographic regions to mitigate the impact of any single investment's performance on your overall portfolio.

4. Practice Patience

Investing is a long-term endeavor, and success often requires patience and perseverance. Avoid succumbing to the temptation of chasing hot stocks for quick gains and focus instead on building a diversified portfolio of high-quality investments designed to deliver sustainable returns over time.

Chasing hot stocks may offer the allure of quick profits, but it often leads to disappointment and losses for investors. By understanding the risks involved, conducting thorough research, sticking to your investment strategy, diversifying your portfolio, and practicing patience, you can avoid the trap of chasing hot stocks and build a more resilient and successful investment portfolio in the long run.

10.2 Ignoring Fees and Taxes

Ignoring fees and taxes is a common mistake that investors often overlook when making investment decisions. In this section, we delve into the importance of considering fees and taxes and offer insights on how to mitigate their impact on investment returns.

Understanding the Impact

Fees and taxes can significantly erode investment returns over time, reducing the overall profitability of an investment portfolio. Ignoring these costs can result in lower net returns and hinder progress toward achieving financial goals.

The Risks Involved

1. High Expense Ratios

Mutual funds and exchange-traded funds (ETFs) often charge management fees, known as expense ratios, which are deducted from investors' returns. High expense ratios can eat into investment returns, especially over the long term, and diminish the compounding effect of investment gains.

2. Trading Commissions

Buying and selling securities through brokerage accounts typically incur trading commissions or fees. Frequent trading activity can result in substantial commission costs, particularly for active traders or investors who engage in short-term trading strategies.

3. Tax Implications

Capital gains taxes on investment profits can reduce overall returns, particularly for investments held in taxable accounts. Ignoring tax implications, such as short-term vs. long-term capital gains rates, can result in unexpected tax liabilities and diminish after-tax returns.

How to Mitigate the Impact

1. Evaluate Investment Costs

Before making investment decisions, carefully evaluate the costs associated with each investment, including management fees, expense ratios, and trading commissions. Choose low-cost investment options, such as index funds or ETFs, to minimize fees and maximize investment returns.

2. Consider Tax-Efficient Investments

Invest in tax-efficient investment vehicles, such as tax-advantaged retirement accounts (e.g., 401(k), IRA) or municipal bonds, to reduce the impact of taxes on investment returns. Utilize tax-loss harvesting strategies to offset capital gains with capital losses and minimize taxable income.

3. Optimize Portfolio Turnover

Minimize portfolio turnover and trading activity to reduce transaction costs and capital gains taxes. Focus on long-term investing and resist the urge to engage in frequent buying and selling of securities, which can incur unnecessary fees and taxes.

4. Consult with a Financial Advisor

Seek advice from a qualified financial advisor who can help you navigate investment costs and tax considerations. A financial advisor can provide personalized recommendations tailored to your financial goals, risk tolerance, and tax situation, helping you optimize investment returns and minimize unnecessary costs.

Ignoring fees and taxes can have a detrimental impact on investment returns and hinder progress toward achieving financial goals. By understanding the impact of investment costs, evaluating fees and taxes, and implementing strategies to mitigate their impact, investors can enhance their investment returns and build wealth more effectively over time. With careful planning, informed decision-making, and proactive management of investment costs and tax implications, investors can optimize their investment portfolios and achieve greater long-term financial success.

10.3 Failing to Plan for the Long Term

Failing to plan for the long term is a common mistake that can hinder investors from achieving their financial goals and building wealth over time. In this section, we explore the importance of long-term planning and offer insights on how to avoid this critical investment mistake.

Understanding the Importance

Planning for the long term is essential for achieving financial security, building wealth, and realizing long-term financial goals. Failing to plan for the future can result in missed opportunities, inadequate savings, and financial instability in retirement or other life stages.

The Risks Involved

1. Short-Term Focus

Focusing solely on short-term investment gains can lead to impulsive decision-making, excessive trading, and a lack of discipline in sticking to a long-term investment strategy. Short-term thinking often results in missed opportunities for compounding returns and wealth accumulation over time.

2. Inadequate Savings

Without a long-term plan in place, investors may fail to save and invest enough to achieve their financial goals, such as retirement savings, education funding, or wealth accumulation objectives. Inadequate savings can leave investors unprepared for future expenses and financial emergencies.

3. Market Volatility

Failing to plan for market volatility and fluctuations can expose investors to unnecessary risk and uncertainty. Without a long-term perspective, investors may panic during market downturns, sell investments at depressed prices, and miss out on potential recovery and long-term growth opportunities.

How to Avoid the Mistake

1. Set Clear Financial Goals

Define your financial goals and objectives for the long term, including retirement savings, education funding, debt reduction, and wealth accumulation targets. Establish clear, measurable goals and create a financial plan to achieve them over time.

2. Develop a Long-Term Investment Strategy

Develop a disciplined, long-term investment strategy based on your financial goals, risk tolerance, and time horizon. Focus on building a diversified portfolio of high-quality investments designed to deliver sustainable returns and mitigate risk over the long term.

3. Practice Patience and Discipline

Stay focused on your long-term investment objectives and resist the temptation to react impulsively to short-term market fluctuations or noise. Practice patience, discipline, and consistency in executing your investment strategy, even during periods of market volatility or uncertainty.

4. Regularly Review and Adjust Your Plan

Regularly review your financial plan and investment strategy to ensure they remain aligned with your long-term goals and objectives. Make adjustments as necessary based on changes in your personal circumstances, financial goals, or market conditions to stay on track toward achieving financial success.

Failing to plan for the long term can have serious consequences for investors, including inadequate savings, missed investment opportunities, and financial insecurity in retirement or other life stages. By recognizing the importance of long-term planning, setting clear financial goals, developing a disciplined investment strategy, practicing patience and discipline, and regularly reviewing and adjusting their plan, investors can position themselves for long-term financial success and achieve their financial goals with greater confidence and peace of mind. With a commitment to long-term planning and prudent decision-making, investors can build wealth steadily over time and secure a brighter financial future for themselves and their families.

Conclusion

Congratulations on completing "Stock Market Investing for Beginners: A Crash Course in Understanding the Basics of the Stock Market in Just 2 Hours"! In this short but comprehensive guide, you've embarked on a journey to demystify the world of stock market investing and gain a solid understanding of its fundamental concepts.

Throughout this crash course, you've learned:

- The basics of the stock market, including what stocks are, how they are traded, and why people invest in them.
- The importance of conducting fundamental analysis to evaluate companies and make informed investment decisions.
- The role of technical analysis in identifying market trends and patterns to guide trading strategies.
- Different types of investments, such as stocks, bonds, mutual funds, ETFs, and index funds, and how to diversify your portfolio for optimal risk management.
- Strategies for building and managing your investment portfolio, including choosing stocks, allocating assets, and rebalancing regularly.
- Key principles for long-term success in investing, including the importance of patience, discipline, and managing emotions and risk effectively.

By arming yourself with this knowledge and adopting a disciplined approach to investing, you're well-equipped to navigate the complexities of the stock market with confidence and resilience. Remember, investing is a journey, not a sprint, and success often requires patience, perseverance, and continuous learning.

As you embark on your investing journey, keep in mind that mistakes are inevitable, but they also present valuable learning opportunities. Stay curious, stay informed, and stay committed to your long-term financial goals. With dedication, diligence, and a sound investment strategy, you have the power to build wealth steadily over time and achieve financial freedom.

Thank you for joining us on this educational adventure. Here to your success and prosperity in the world of stock market investing!

Happy investing!

www.ingramcontent.com/pod-product-compliance
Lightning Source LLC
Chambersburg PA
CBHW082107220526
45472CB00009B/2087